World War 1 Heroes

*Unforgettable Tales of Courage,
Selflessness, and Resilience*

Table of Contents

Introduction

First World War history often gets categorized into the actions of nations, heads of state, and institutions, but you seldom hear the names of the battlefield heroes who bravely put their all into achieving their ideals. WWI profoundly shaped the current society and laid the foundations for WWII. Furthermore, the first modern war redefined warfare in many ways. The war's global chess pieces, moved by powerful individuals, caused many people on the front lines and in pivotal positions to remain faceless and nameless. The grand narrative swallows their actions, but without their participation, the cogs of war don't spin.

There were no clear good and bad guys in the First World War, which resulted from European nations competing for power. Millions of people needlessly died in a war that diplomatic efforts and sound reasoning could have avoided. Germany and Austria-Hungary are often mentioned as the main instigators of the war, but many interlocking and complex parts led to the first bombs being dropped. With the invention of aviation and the rapid advancement of weaponry technology, WWI was more devastating than the preceding wars. It was often called *the war to end all wars* because it was the first time many nations worldwide were in active conflict.

The leading players were the Entente Powers (The Allies), which included France, Russia, Italy, the British Empire, and the United States, against the Central Powers, headed by the German Empire, the Austrian-Hungarian Empire, and the Ottoman Empire. World War I could be seen as the beginning of the end of the imperial age as empires split into nation-states at the end of the war. It was the starting point of world governance as the League of Nations was established to facilitate global peace.

However, this lofty goal was not achieved because Germany was forced to pay reparations for its financial support of Austria-Hungary at the start of the war, without which the conflict likely would not have commenced. This laid the foundation for WWII because the German economy collapsed, and the Germans felt humiliated, which opened the doorway for a strong nationalistic leader to emerge.

Through these civilization-shifting events, still relevant today, brilliant individuals emerged previously lost in the collective narrative. This book highlights their triumphs and tribulations to give honor to the heroes of WWI. By exploring their stories, history comes alive. *You have a front-row seat into the lives of incredibly resilient people who built the world you live in today with their heroic efforts and sacrifices.*

Chapter 1: Manfred von Richthofen's Skyward Mastery

Trench warfare necessitated combat to be taken to the skies. This meant that pilots became the envied heroes. Manfred von Richthofen stands out among many of these brave men. His dedication and skill made him a beast in the air whom no enemy pilot would ever want to encounter. The number of victories he stacked up is a testament to his ferociously deadly trigger finger.

Manfred von Richthofen is also known as the "Red Baron."
Cassowary Colorizations, CC BY 2.0 <https://creativecommons.org/licenses/by/2.0>, via Wikimedia Commons:
https://commons.wikimedia.org/wiki/File:Manfred_von_Richthofen_%22The_Red_Baron%22_in_Schweidnitz,_1918_(26739402207).jpg

Nothing ignites the imagination more than the high-octane dog fights that dominated the skies over WWI's Western and Eastern fronts. The whizzing acrobatics spurred on by beating propellers induce visions of glory or bursting into terrifying flames, depending on whether you are on the winning or losing side. Manfred von Richthofen was arguably the best pilot of the numerous heroes who sat in a cockpit. By the fatal end of his two-year career, he had shot down 80 enemy aircraft, becoming the highest tallying fighter in the war. His precision flying, fearlessness, and unbridled bravery were a double-edged sword that stoked his glory but led to his untimely demise.

Von Richthofen's combat success and humble, respectable demeanor off the battlefield made him a model warrior. German authorities soon realized this and used his image as a tool to motivate troops and garner support for their warfare goals. Moreover, the gentleman warrior gained respect among his peers and enemies. He earned the highest decorations in the German military and was honored by the Allied forces in death. Myths evolved around his story, with word spreading that the British Forces had put a bounty on his head and would award any soldier who brought him down with a Victoria Cross. When truth and fiction are separated, von Richthofen stands strong as a man dedicated to his duty who would do all he could to uplift his fellow soldiers.

Retelling his unique story, you will see how unbreakable focus and dedication can lead to the highest heights of achievement. Von Richthofen was not an academic or philosophical thinker. He was the practical everyman who went forth with intuitive ambition. The mastery of his aircraft could not be taught but is rather a drive embedded deep inside the souls of unbreakable and dedicated people. His perfect combination of confidence and humility created the deadly combination that made him unstoppable in the air. His bright three-winged plane will forever be engraved into the minds of those familiar with the details of the WWI conflict.

Rise of the Red Baron

The German pilot was one of the deadliest fliers in the war. He was nicknamed "the Red Baron" due to the flamboyantly painted aircraft he flew and his upbringing as a Prussian aristocrat. Knees knocked, and teeth chattered when the Red Baron was seen approaching from the horizon. Any wise pilot knew they were in for a terrible fight. The unparalleled skill of von Richthofen grew his legend as the best ace in the war. Between 1916 and 1918, he shot down 80 Allied planes with surgical precision. No one else reached this incredibly high number of hits on enemy aircraft.

Von Richthofen earned his pilot license on the western front of the war. After flying several combat missions in France and Russia, the Red Baron met the German ace Oswald Boelcke, who took him under his wing and taught von Richthofen how to fly at an elite level. Von Richthofen was a natural fighter pilot who quickly earned the title "flying ace," meaning a fighter had shot down five or more enemy aircraft. Von Richthofen shot down his first plane on September 17, 1916. Early the following year, he had already racked up 16 confirmed enemy takedowns. During this period, von Richthofen's brilliant flying earned him the German military medal, Pour le Mérite.

After recognizing his unmatched talent, the German military put von Richthofen in charge of the squadron, Jasta 11 (Jagdstaffel 11), which included Lothar von Richthofen, the Red Baron's younger brother. The team was a cohesive unit of adept pilots going on multiple successful missions. As the commander of Jasta 11, the self-confident pilot sprayed his Albatross D.III fighter plane scarlet-red, birthing the Red Baron nickname that would live on for generations. Some of his other nicknames included "The Red Knight," "le Petit Rouge," and "The Red Battle Flier." You can bet a million dollars that when enemy fighters saw that blood-red plane approaching in the distance, they shivered with fear because they knew the terror they were in for.

Unlike many commanders in his time, von Richthofen flew in the front lines of battle, leading his squadron multiple times a day. The commander felt at home in the seat of his beloved red aircraft that carried him through numerous sticky situations into victory before meeting his crashing end. He believed he could not expect those under his command to perform if he did not show them how. Von Richthofen was an old-school leader who did not craft strategy and then handed it over to others to execute. His success shows that he loved being in the heat of battle because of his passion for combat flying and sense of duty to his country.

As the Red Baron continuously emerged victorious after multiple close calls, his allies and enemies saw him as undefeatable. He continued his reign of precision shooting until he was gunned down in 1918. It seems fitting that he met his end being shot down by gunners on the ground after swooping low because nobody could defeat him in the sky. His military prowess in the air could not be replicated because, although he may not have been the greatest academically, he was certainly a genius in the cockpit. Von Richthofen had so much impact in only two years as a fighter pilot that when the body of the young 25-year-old was found by Allied fighters, he was buried with military honors by enemy soldiers. The legend of the Red Baron lived on after the war, with his story being told through multiple media, including song, television, and comic books.

Early Military Career

Von Richthofen's military career began early in his life when his wealthy family sent him to military school in Wahlstatt at the tender age of 11. He graduated from the Royal Prussian Main Cadet Institute (Preußische Hauptkadettenanstalt), the main military academy training officer corps of the Prussian Army, excelling at sports but not so much at academics. As his military career progressed, he joined Russia's Uhlan regiment as part of cavalry reconnaissance. His unit fought in Russia, France, and Belgium at the beginning of the war. The cavalry unit eventually disbanded due to the trench warfare that defined WWI, making them obsolete. In addition to his role in the cavalry, von Richthofen served as a messenger on the Eastern and Western fronts.

His noble background explains why the decorated pilot was committed to honor and duty. His affluent family groomed him from a young age to enter the military. The ideological value system he held was drilled into his mind before he could understand the implications of adopting such unwavering principles. He was destined to become a war hero from early on, but it is doubtful that anybody could have predicted how lethal he would be behind the aircraft's controls. His practical and hands-on nature perfectly gelled with being a pilot, as if he were born for the position. Von Richthofen's commitment to perfecting his abilities and learning from everybody allowed him to rise as the war's best fighter pilot.

Before joining the German Air Service, von Richthofen flew supplies in the war. He asked to be transferred because he felt his potential was wasted in the supply branch. It was one of his best decisions because he was a natural at air fights. Before he flew in the Air Service as a pilot, he began as an observer on Feldfliegerabteilung 69 aircraft. His journey to becoming an ace started when he was assigned to the pilot, Oswald

Boelcke, who would teach him many skills that would make him a hero. He eventually surpassed his mentor and became popularly known as the "ace of aces."

Von Richthofen looked up to Boelcke, worshiping the ground he walked on. Boelcke had crafted a reputation as one of the best aces and was described by many as the "Father of Air Combat." Von Richthofen once described how he saw himself as a great fighter pilot, but he could not match Boelcke's heroism. Oswald Boelcke's expertise was respected throughout the ranks of the military, so much so that he distributed an instructional manual throughout the German Air Service for pilots to learn the principles that made him successful in combat.

Before becoming a pilot, von Richthofen fought bravely in the trenches, bobbing and weaving along the front lines as a messenger. Von Richthofen moved like a ninja, ducking and diving as enemy bullets zipped past his helmet. He was awarded the Iron Cross for his heroic performance on the battlefield. Slowly, aircraft took over as the predominant battle strategy due to the damage they caused in the trenches. This may be why von Richthofen was so eager to get into the air fights. However, the Red Baron's rise to the top was not without obstacles. The decorated pilot crashed in his first solo fight, but he persisted until he was recruited to Boelcke's Jasta II squadron – when the combat legend recognized the potential of the young, up-and-coming pilot. Without Boelcke, it is unlikely that von Richthofen would have reached the heights he did in air combat.

Leader of the Flying Circus

As von Richthofen rose through the ranks, he became the commander of the new Jasta 11 squadron of the German Air Service. Von Richthofen went on to become even more successful, eventually rising to commander of the larger wing of the air service, Jagdgeschwader 1, which was made up of multiple squadrons. By the time he commanded this leadership role, his legend was being spread far and wide. Von Richthofen was the perfect poster child for German propaganda and was used as a national symbol to gain war bonds. A handsome pilot who was feared and respected was the perfect candidate to promote the war effort. Von Richthofen's blood-red three-winged Fokker Dr.I Triplane (that he flew as the commander of the Flying Circus) has made many pop culture appearances and is still an iconic symbol of the First World War.

The Fokker Dr.I Triplane.

The Red Baron became the commander of Jasta 11 when he completed his 16th kill. After stepping into this leadership role as commander of Jasta 11, von Richthofen's deadly streak would continue, ending up with a tally of 52 victories. April 1917 was a notable month because, in thirty days, von Richthofen defeated 22 British fighters. His commitment and unparalleled accomplishments put von Richthofen at the front of the queue to command Jagdgeschwader 1, a combination of the Jasta 4, 6, 10, and 11 squadrons. He committed to training the elite pilots, and many became commanders of their squadrons.

Part of von Richthofen's units' successes can be credited to him emphasizing pride in your team and position. This pride was not only expressed verbally but was also enforced by actions. For example, von Richthofen encouraged the pilots under his command to paint personalized pictures onto their aircraft to feel more like their own and establish a personal connection with the vehicle that propelled them onto the edge of life and death. As much as he encouraged the members of his squadron, he was by far the most valued member of the team. Von Richthofen spoke about how he never got into a plane for frivolous folly, so he would shoot to kill, aiming for the head of the pilot or the observer. German General Erich Ludendorff praised von Richthofen, noting that as an individual, he had as much worth as three squadrons.

Von Richthofen saw his primary purpose as the wing commander, ensuring the mission was completed. Secondly, he had to teach his team members so they could unlock their full potential in the dangerous skies. Von Richthofen believed in celebrating victories to boost morale and self-esteem. He knew that small successes were the steps to achieve greatness. Winning is like a drug; the more you win, the more you want to win. Von Richthofen took full advantage of this human psychology by building his team brick – by brick. He applied the same principle to himself by getting a silver cup engraved every time he shot an enemy out of the sky. The tradition ended when his jeweler ran out of silver because all metals were being contributed to the war effort, and by that time, von Richthofen had already gained sixty cups.

The Flying Circus's success was one of Germany's greatest propaganda tools. Von Richthofen had become so famous and interwoven with the imagery of the war that top officials feared his death would demoralize the populace. The squadron's nickname came from a combination of their aesthetics and function. The unit could quickly dispatch to wherever they were needed and often set up tents in various locations. They had distinctive, brightly colored planes. Their traveling, coupled with the colors, resulted in them getting called The Flying Circus, a brilliant branding tool that could be easily used for promotions.

Aerial Battles

Von Richthofen avoided the fancy twisting and turning the British fighters were accustomed to. He flew efficiently straight to his target to gun them down. Instead of relying on the skills of one individual pilot, German fighters flew in formation. Von Richthofen understood that in the air, all that mattered were results. Therefore, he targeted slow-flying two-seaters with their fuel tanks in the rear so he could easily gun them down. Getting rid of easy targets quickly resulted in von Richthofen's victories skyrocketing.

Instead of conforming to the status quo, von Richthofen embraced more effective tactics. He cut off the tricky frills of flying that many other pilots gravitated toward, only opting to do what was necessary. By abandoning needless tricks, he promoted deadly precision that had never been seen before. Von Richthofen flew through the air like a predator, turning opponents into prey as he relentlessly chased them down. His legend was embraced as part of the American military's mythology. The Peanuts cartoon had already immortalized the Red

Baron. Hence, many soldiers used iconography, carving a tired snoopy being chased by the Red Baron onto their planes and equipment during the Vietnam War. The pictures would include quirky quotes like "Good grief, another mission." Decades after his death, his battle perseverance was still referenced.

The precision flying and teamwork of The Flying Circus is what led to von Richthofen's most successful era. They chased down and killed enemies while staying in disciplined formation. The Allied forces did not know how to deal with their skilled marksmanship and exceptional piloting abilities that deviated from the dogfight norms of the day. Von Richthofen applied many of Boelcke's tactics but was far more actively involved than his respected mentor, choosing to lead from the front.

Some controversy is attached to the brilliance of von Richthofen. His ruthless efficiency would inspire the fighting style of the Nazis in WWII. Furthermore, Hermann Göring, who would become one of the most powerful and notorious Nazi leaders, commanded the same Flying Circus squadron as von Richthofen. Although tactically, they used similar strategies, von Richthofen was long gone before the genocidal regime took over.

Personal Ethos

Although von Richthofen brutally killed many of his enemies by shooting their fuel tanks and causing them to burn to death, he had a reputation for humble chivalry when he stepped out of the pilot's seat. Von Richthofen worked incredibly hard on his skills because he heavily respected his enemies. Anyone who stepped onto the battlefield to fight for their country earned his respect, and his ruthlessness in the skies ensured that he was equally respected and feared.

Von Richthofen is the ultimate warrior because, coupled with his deadly and ruthless decision-making on the battlefield, he had a gentlemanly attitude. He was always respectful to those in his command, stoically controlling his emotions and never losing his temper. He understood that to build unity, you must have respect; otherwise, your fellow airmen will not be motivated to give their all in the mission. Most of von Richthofen's actions were driven by ambition, so he had to connect with his squadron to get the best out of them. Hence, he always treated them with dignity.

The Red Baron never allowed his focus to be broken until the tragic end of his life. He had close calls during his flying career, sustaining life-changing injuries. When it was suggested that he join the ground forces due to a head injury, which was causing him nausea and migraines, von Richthofen refused because the ordinary soldier did not have the luxury of choosing his position. So, out of principle and duty, he felt obliged to keep flying. This choice eventually led to his untimely demise at 25 years old: The Red Baron was shot out of the sky by someone on the ground as he attempted to evade enemy fire. His death adds to the mystique of his legend because even when he was finally defeated, it was not by another pilot.

In many ways, von Richthofen was a paradox. He was the most deadly enemy fighter, but the Allied forces gave him an honorable funeral. He had a humble demeanor coupled with unmatched self-confidence. While a war hero, he inspired some of the most evil men who would rise to power in WWII. Through all these contradictions, the Red Baron emerges as one of the most enigmatic figures of the First World War. His pride, skill, loyalty, and perseverance are branded into the flesh of the first global conflict so that his memory as a battlefield hero cannot be erased. When WWI dogfights are brought up, Manfred von Richthofen will echo into eternity as the greatest fighter pilot of his era.

Chapter 2: Lawrence of Arabia: The Desert Warrior

Thomas Edward Lawrence, aka Lawrence of Arabia, is a name that has echoed through the ages. Even those unfamiliar with history have probably heard about him since he was immortalized in various movies and TV shows. Lawrence will live forever in the hearts and minds of the British and the Arabs. He was the hero who fought with the Arabs, liberated them from the Ottoman Empire, and helped them stand on their feet again.

The Lawrence of Arabia.
https://commons.wikimedia.org/wiki/File:Te_lawrence.jpg

This chapter covers the story of British and revolutionary officer Thomas Edward Lawrence and how he orchestrated the Arab Revolt against the Ottoman forces.

Who Was Thomas Edward Lawrence?

Lawrence was born in Wales in the United Kingdom on August 16, 1888. Unlike most children his age who spent their time playing and having fun with their friends, Lawrence was interested in antiques, monuments, and architecture. In 1910, he graduated with a history degree from Jesus College, Oxford. Afterward, he worked as an archaeologist in Syria, Palestine, and Egypt when they were under the Ottoman Empire's reign. In 1914, he served in the intelligence staff of the British Middle East Command in Cairo, which witnessed the first campaign against the Ottoman Empire. In 1916, he was posted to Saudi Arabia, where he became a famous legend and changed the course of history. During his time with the Arabs, Lawrence became fluent in Arabic, which helped him understand the Arabs, whom he came to respect and admire.

Lawrence was a liaison officer between the Arabs and the British. The British government wanted the Arabs to revolt against the Ottoman Empire, so they sent him to offer their assistance to the people.

Although other British officers were working with the Arabs, Lawrence was the most famous. He was one of the few officers who didn't only rely on his military skills but established close relationships with some of the Arab leaders. Lawrence was one of the youngest and least experienced British officers, but his respect for the Arabs and their culture made him a great success.

Lawrence was often described as a "man divided" because he was a British officer loyal to the crown who came to the Middle East on behalf of his government. He was ordered to study the Arabs and learn everything about them. He was supposed to infiltrate them to discover their vulnerabilities to control them. However, Lawrence was eating their food, speaking their language, and dressing like them. He couldn't help but feel that he was among family and friends. He even felt guilty for failing to negotiate their freedom after the war.

Lawrence's Tactical Expertise in Guerrilla Warfare and Battle Strategies

Guerrilla warfare tactics are unconventional and indirect battlefield techniques that involve hit and run, ambushes, raids, and sabotage, usually carried out by paramilitary people, armed civilians, or rebels.

Lawrence spent a long time in the desert with the Bedouins (Arabic-speaking nomadic tribes living in the desert), where he gained his tactical expertise. Since Lawrence was a military expert, he believed the Arabs could win the war without engaging in direct battle. He suggested they use guerrilla warfare.

Guerrilla warfare was the perfect strategy for people who didn't have enough men, weapons, or resources to engage in regular battle. Lawrence prepared a small group of Arab tribesmen to attack the Ottoman army. His plan was to prepare the smallest group to attack at the farthest point from them and in the quickest way. It was a hit-and-run tactic, one of the many techniques of guerrilla warfare. Lawrence called this war "The Wall of Detachment" because it brought the biggest losses to the Turks, with only a few Arab casualties.

Welsh writer Phil Carradice described Lawrence's guerrilla warfare tactics as "the stuff of legend," especially his capture of Aqaba.

Lawrence was a self-disciplined, tough warrior. He went days without water, food, and sleep to test his strength and see how long he could go without the necessities. Unsurprisingly, Winston Churchill described him as "One of the greatest men that ever lived."

Lawrence's Skills in Sabotage

Since the Turkish army was spread across the large Arabian Desert, it was easy for the Hejaz rebels (modern-day Saudi Arabia) to attack the Ottoman army and destroy their supply and communication lines. The British controlled the Red Sea, so the Turks were forced to use the Hejaz railway to transport their weapons, supplies, and men.

With Lawrence's help, the Arabs spent two years sabotaging parts of the Hejaz railway. He had a brilliant plan to surprise and trick the Turks. He sent a small group of men to sabotage the tracks. While the Turkish army defended themselves, he gathered a large group of men to perform fast hit-and-run tactics.

Lawrence's guerrilla techniques worked to weaken the enemy lines. He used fewer men for his attacks than the Turks did to defend the tracks. His attacks were severe as he preferred to use explosives since they brought the most extensive damage and required the most and longest repairs. One of Lawrence's favorite explosives was the "Tulip Bomb," which twisted the tracks, rendering them irreparable.

Another tactic Lawrence often used was to drive the tracks out of service. He sent 20 men to remove the rails and throw them away, and blew up bridges to shatter instead of crumbling so they would take longer to fix.

All these tactics were difficult to execute. For instance, blowing up trains was challenging, but Lawrence devised a way by laying explosives alongside the tracks with someone firing at them from a distance.

Lawrence also brought modern weapons to the Arabs, like bi-planes. These weapons gave them an advantage. The Arabs were also introduced to Rolls Royce armored cars and motorcycles, which many had never seen before.

Lawrence showed the Arabs the power of his modern weapons by striking a railway with one of his armored cars. In 1917, he drove another armored car at 60mph to attack the Turkish garrison. He surprised and defeated his enemies. He referred to fighting with modern weapons as "Fighting Deluxe."

Lawrence showed his military genius by combining modern and traditional strategies and weapons.

Lawrence's Relationship with Arab Leaders

Lawrence knew he couldn't win this war with his military skills alone. He needed to develop diplomatic skills. Hence, he established strong bonds with Emir Feisal, the son of Sharif Hussein of Mecca, one of the most significant leaders in the Arab region. Lawrence was clever, charismatic, and influential. He convinced Feisal and Abdullah I, King of Jordan, to support Britain against the Ottoman Empire. The Arabs trusted him, and together, they planned various guerrilla attacks that gave them an advantage over their enemies.

Although he had a good relationship with most Arab leaders, he considered Feisal a good friend. Lawrence spent two years in Hejaz with Feisal and recognized him as the strongest Arab leader in the revolution against the Turks. With his trusted friend's help, he created an Arab army supported and funded by the British.

Lawrence and Prince Feisal met in 1917 when Lawrence was sent to determine if the Arabs needed assistance in their revolution against the Turks. He was ordered to find a clever, strong man to lead the Arabs in battle. Lawrence believed Sharif to be the right man for the job. However, when Lawrence got to know him better, he found him stubborn and inflexible, so he preferred his son, Feisal, over him. In his memoirs, he wrote that he knew from the first moment that Feisal was the man he had come to find. He possessed the leadership qualities and skills to lead the Arabs to victory.

Feisal had many other admirable qualities like ambition, flexibility, and efficiency, and Lawrence believed he had what it would take to start the Arab Revolt. Feisal admired Lawrence and found him faithful, well-connected, and clever. Lawrence had money, gold, and access to some of the most expensive weapons in the world, thanks to the British government. Feisal believed that all of Lawrence's resources would convince other Arab leaders to join him in the revolution.

In battle, Lawrence saw Feisal as level-headed and a problem solver. He would often observe him from his tent and respected how he treated his soldiers with patience and understanding.

Both men had one common goal and were working together to achieve it. Feisal's army respected Lawrence and often sought his advice. They welcomed his suggestions and jumped at the idea of performing guerrilla techniques.

So, why did the Arab leaders trust Lawrence more than any other British officer? Lawrence genuinely cared about the Arab movement and wanted to help free them from Ottoman rule. He adapted to their culture, stayed with them, dressed like them, and spoke their language, and many Arabs regarded him as one of their own.

Once, when Lawrence arrived in Arabia, Feisal gave him a camel as a gift. The prince asked his good friend to ride it and accompany him to Wadi Ais. However, Lawrence had never ridden a camel before. Yet he didn't hesitate and mounted as if he had been riding a camel for years. He also dressed as an Arab in a thobe and a ghutra. The tribesmen who saw him were surprised. An Englishman was dressing and riding like them. He wasn't scared of the strange desert and never complained about riding all day. He never stopped to drink unless they did. They never felt he was a foreigner; he was one of them. Not just another ally but an Arab who just looked and spoke differently.

General Sir Edmund Allenby, commander-in-chief of the Allied Egyptian Expeditionary Force, described Lawrence as loyal to the Arabs. He also credited him as the main force behind the Arab Revolution.

Lawrence's Most Significant Battles and Strategies

Lawrence had proven himself to be a brilliant military leader. It wasn't only the guerrilla tactics that earned him this reputation but also his success in many battles, like the battle of Aqaba, that have made him a legend to this day.

Lawrence's First Raid

In 1917, Lawrence and the Arab Army went on their first raid in the desert. They arrived at a hill opposite a Turkish camp. The army destroyed the camp and took Turkish prisoners. This was the first victory the Arabs achieved against the Turks, with many more to follow.

The Battle of Aqaba

Aqaba was a port city in Jordan where one of the most influential battles between the Arabs and the Turks occurred. Lawrence and Feisal often attended meetings to discuss their next moves against the Turks. In one meeting, Lawrence brought Feisal a very bold plan. The Turks had dozens of navy ships guarding Aqaba from the seaside. So, Lawrence proposed that a group of Arab soldiers cross the desert and attack Aqaba from the landside since it was less fortified. Lawrence believed that controlling the city would put extra pressure on the Ottoman army and allow the British to send aid to their Arab allies. Feisal liked the plan and was ready to attack Aqaba.

Lawrence and Syrian tribe leader Auda Abu Tayih led a troop of 50 Arabs and headed to Aqaba. It was a risky venture. Even Lawrence's British superiors didn't approve and wanted him to wait. However, the Arab army proved them wrong. They caused severe losses to the enemy lines by creating diversions or blowing up railroad tracks.

Lawrence brought 22,000 British gold bars to entice soldiers from different tribes to join them. He expanded his army to 500 men. After a long journey that lasted for two months, Lawrence and the Arab army arrived in Aqaba.

The Turks were severely outnumbered and frightened as they didn't expect the Arab army to be massive. Following Lawrence's orders and strategies, the Turks were surrounded, and the Arabs shot at them from every direction. However, the Arabs failed to cause significant damage to the Turks, frustrating Lawrence. Moreover, it was a scorching hot day, and Lawrence suffered from heat exhaustion (although some said he was only pretending), so he left his post to get some water.

Auda was angry with Lawrence and scolded him for abandoning his post. However, Lawrence snapped at him and said that Auda's men had been shooting for hours and had only hit a couple of Turks. Although Auda felt insulted, Lawrence's words motivated him and his men to get on their horses and camels and attack the Turks viciously. When Lawrence rejoined them, they were shooting at the Turks, but they were more determined this time than ever. They defeated the Turks, killing many and taking the rest as prisoners.

The Battle of Tafilah

Tafilah was a city that connected Amman with the Red Sea. The battle of Tafilah shifted the tide of the war in the Middle East. During the battle, Lawrence and the Arab armies destroyed an Ottoman battalion. Lawrence followed his famous battle strategy by causing severe damage to the enemy's army, killing thousands of Turks and only losing 50 men. This battle earned Lawrence great recognition, and he was awarded the Distinguished Service Order.

Lawrence's efforts and military success in both battles showed the Arabs he was the right man to lead them to victory.

Lawrence and Bedouin Culture

The Bedouins, Bedu in Arabic, are Arabs who live in the desert. They come from many Arab countries like Egypt, Libya, Tunisia, Algeria, Sudan, Morocco, Yemen, Iraq, Saudi Arabia, Jordan, Palestine, and Syria.

Lawrence spent two years with the Bedouins, learning about their culture. He used this knowledge to build trust among the tribe leaders. Judging from the notes he left behind, he was interested in them and their lives. In his notebook, he described a dinner he shared with them in detail, describing the shape of the rugs, the color of the coffee, and the size of the utensils. The detailed description reflected Lawrence's fascination with the Bedouins and their culture.

Lawrence influenced the Bedouins and turned them from nomadic tribes roaming aimlessly in the Arabian Desert to a strong guerrilla army that fought and defeated the Turks. In addition to the Battle of Aqaba, the Bedouins played a significant role in many other major battles.

Although Lawrence had a strong character, he knew he couldn't win the proud Bedouin over by ordering them around. Instead, he earned their respect by being a courageous warrior who inspired them in battle.

Lawrence trusted the Bedouins, and he succeeded in earning their trust. He wrote 27 tips inspired by his interactions and life with them to help other British officers who came into contact with them.

Lawrence's Tips about the Bedouins

- Work on your first impression and watch everything you say and do until you gain the trust of a tribe. Then you can do as you please.
- Avoid giving them directions or orders. Your only job is to advise their tribe chief.
- Don't converse with a Bedouin until you are better acquainted with them and their culture to avoid misunderstandings.
- Treat your sub-chief kindly, but understand you aren't on the same level.
- Treat the tribe leaders respectfully, and they will treat you the same way.
- Be humble and maintain a calm and polite demeanor.
- Call everyone by their name except for the Sharif. Call him "Sidi."
- Hold on to your sense of humor. You will need it.

Lawrence stated that his guidelines applied not only to the Bedouins but to all mankind, for they are universal truths.

After the war and Lawrence's return to Britain, he presented records detailing his experience in the Middle East. He included his adventures with the Bedouins, reflecting their impact on him. He also used his fame to advocate for them.

Lawrence Bedouin Attire

If you look at pictures of Lawrence, he will usually be wearing traditional Bedouin attire. It was rare for a British soldier to let go of his uniform and adopt the clothes of a new culture. However, Lawrence was no ordinary man. When American writer Lowell Thomas published pictures of him in his Bedouin attire, the British public was filled with interest and curiosity. Everyone wanted to know what prompted a British officer to dress this way.

The painting of Lawrence shows him wearing Bedouin attire.
https://commons.wikimedia.org/wiki/File:Painting_of_Lawrence_of_Arabia_by_Augustus_John.jpg

Lawrence said that Prince Feisal suggested he wear Arab clothes. The prince explained that this attire would make him more comfortable, and he would experience the Arabs' traditional dress. Feisal told him that tribe leaders would relate to him if he dressed like them. They would trust and treat him like one of their own.

Lawrence didn't hesitate and dressed as the Arabs he grew to love. It was a sign of respect and admiration for Arab traditions and customs.

Officers today can learn so much from Lawrence. They should study his guerrilla warfare techniques and learn how he used them to defeat his enemies. However, one of Lawrence's biggest accomplishments was establishing a relationship with the Arabs. During wars, people detach themselves from others to avoid situations that could cloud their judgments. But Lawrence focused on getting close to people, and they became his friends and trusted allies. Whether he genuinely cared about the Arabs or only faked it to follow orders, no one can deny that Lawrence succeeded on and off the battlefield and became a legend.

The story of Lawrence of Arabia will live forever: The British soldier torn between his duty and the people with whom he connected and genuinely cared about.

Chapter 3: Edith Cavell: The Angel of Mercy behind Enemy Lines

This chapter chronicles the bravery of Nurse Edith Cavell in occupied Belgium, discussing her role in establishing a network to help over 200 Allied soldiers escape, her dedication to treating wounded soldiers regardless of nationality, and her eventual capture and execution. Beyond the international outcry over her death and its impact on wartime sentiment, you'll learn about her unique philosophy on nursing as a duty transcending national loyalties and how it influenced her decision-making during the war.

Nurse Edith Cavell played a role in the escape of 200 Allied soldiers.
https://commons.wikimedia.org/wiki/File:Edith_Cavell.jpg

Early Life of Edith Cavell

A daughter of a vicar, Edith Cavell was raised with strong moral values, which determined her path in life. She was born in 1865 in Swardeston, the eldest of four children. After finishing school, she sought employment as a governess. She worked with several families, first in the United Kingdom and then in Belgium, and her employers remarked on her compassionate and loving nature. In 1895, she nursed her father back to health from a serious ailment, during which she found her true vocation: nursing. Soon after, she entered the nursing staff at the Royal London Hospital in Whitechapel and was trained under one of Florence Nightingale's colleagues and friends, Matron Eva Lückes. Upon completing her training, she worked in several British hospitals. When she returned to Brussels to care for a friend's sick child, Cavell was already well known in Belgium, and her fame and experience earned her an invitation to become the matron of Belgium's first official nursing school, L'École Belge d'Infirmières Diplômées. By 1910, Edith Cavell was a training nurse in numerous schools, kindergartens, and hospitals across Belgium and launched the prominent nursing journal L'infirmière.

World War I

Cavell learned about the beginnings of World War I while she was visiting her mother in the United Kingdom. Before the war reached Belgium, she was already back in Brussels, offering her services as a nurse wherever needed. Although she temporarily left her position as a mistress of the nursing school, she would soon return. Moreover, she sent her German and Dutch students home, knowing they were needed there, just as she was needed by the injured in Belgium.

On August 4, Britain, supported by Russia and France (the three countries were known as the Allies and their troops as the Allied soldiers), declared war on Germany, and the war reached Belgium. As the German soldiers invaded Brussels, the injured poured into the institution where Edith Cavell worked. After being urged by Dr. Antoine Depage, the school's founder and main patron, Edith returned to the L'École Belge d'Infirmières Diplômées. The school served as a Red Cross Hospital, taking in wounded soldiers from all sides, Allied and invaders. Cavell took them in her stride, caring for each, regardless of nationality. She encouraged other nurses not to be preferential, considering their duty to care for the injured lives the most important, irrespective of the circumstances.

While some British nurses returned home before the Battle of Mons, Cavell and her faithful assistant Nurse Wilkins remained, caring for the wounded. As the battle began on August 23, the British soldiers soon realized they were outnumbered and were forced to retreat. However, during the hasty retreat, confusion arose, and many British soldiers were cut off from the safety route. While they initially found shelters with local Samaritans, the Germans soon discovered their locations and executed them and the people who harbored them.

Escape Organization

Seeing them as neutral parties, the Germans were not concerned about Edith Cavell or other British nurses working with her. However, they realized these nurses cared for German soldiers with as much compassion as the wounded from the Belgian or Allied troops. It was a decision they would later regret because Edith Cavell and her nurses were not as neutral or impartial as they seemed to be.

Cavell learned about British soldiers being cut off behind the enemy lines when two arrived at her training school. They were injured and in need of shelter, so Cavell did what she considered the right thing to do and allowed them to hide there for two weeks, despite knowing what would happen if the Germans learned of it. Besides this, she helped them cross the border to neighboring Netherlands, a neutral country. Soon, other British soldiers learned about this refuge and the possible aid for slipping across the border, and when they knocked at the school's door (using the password "yorc"), they were aided to safety. Cavell asked one of the soldiers from the Norfolk Regiment, whom she sent to the Dutch border, to deliver a letter in her name for her mother in Norfolk.

Soon, Edith Cavell became one of the key players in a complex underground lifeline established for the Allied refugees. Prince Reginald de Croÿ aided their efforts by offering his home, Château de Bellignies in France, as a shelter and meeting point. He provided the Allied soldiers with false papers and set them on their way to shelters in Brussels, including Nurse Cavell's training school. Cavell and the others who volunteered to shelter the refugees provided them with enough money and supplies to reach the border, where additional guides awaited them. The refugees were guided from Brussels by men like Philippe

Baucq, who, with the help of Edith Cavell, helped 200 Allied soldiers find safety beyond the German occupation line. Edith and her comrades continued this underground operation for a staggering nine months before things went awry.

In the meantime, Edith Cavell and her nurses faced a double dilemma. For one, as employers of the Red Cross, they were supposed to remain neutral parties in a war, which they certainly weren't anymore. Moreover, if the Germans learned about them harboring Allied soldiers, they would be killed without question. In the end, when weighing the consequences of sacrificing her conscience and possibly her life against the act of guiding people to safety, Edith decided to stay true to the latter. She was a true humanitarian at heart, and beyond caring for all nationalities, she considered the protection and concealment of those in mortal danger a just and moral cause.

While she recorded her dilemmas in her diary (which she kept in her pillow), Nurse Cavell left no traces of her illegal activities. Even when a Belgian informant to the Germans searched her training school (by this time, the Germans weren't as clueless about the refugee lines as Cavell and the other hosts thought they were), she remained calm and poised because she knew they wouldn't find any incriminating evidence against her or her nurses. The latter were not informed of Cavell's activities so they wouldn't be incriminated. While they noticed she had become withdrawn, her colleagues only thought Cavell was preoccupied with the war's events.

She was concerned about juggling the underground operation (she had to find more ways to finance it) and continuing to run her training school as usual so as not to cause suspicion. She was also tasked to oversee the building of a new nursing school. Yet, despite all her obligations, she was determined to continue helping the refugees. Moreover, when the patrons of her school learned about the Germans' suspicion of her harboring Allied soldiers and helping them escape, they expressed grave concern.

Arrest and Imprisonment

From the moment the German authorities suspected Edith Cavell's involvement in the underground operations against German military law, she was under heavy scrutiny. Eventually, she was betrayed by a French collaborator, Georges Gaston Quien, and arrested along with numerous refugee hosts. Following a grueling 72-hour interrogation, during which the German soldiers spared no means to intimidate her, Cavell admitted aiding almost 200 Allied soldiers in their attempt to reach the safety of the Dutch frontier after sheltering them for weeks at a time.

However, her confession was obtained through trickery. On August 8, 1915, Cavell was told that she only needed to confirm her involvement (indicating they already had this information), and if she did, her allies would be spared. She believed the German investigators, signed her confession, and was transferred to Brussels's famous Saint Gilles prison, where she spent 10 weeks, including 14 days in solitary confinement.

By the end of August, the American Ambassador in Belgium, Brand Whitlock, had learned about Cavell's imprisonment and promptly inquired about the charges against her. However, Baron von der Lancken, the German political minister stationed in Brussels who received the letter, didn't reply. During her 10-week incarceration, Edith Cavell wrote several letters to her school and family. She received flowers and embroidery material from her fellow nurses so she would have something to occupy herself within her lonely holding cell. While initially uneasy about leaving behind the scurry of activity she was used to throughout her life, Cavell reportedly found the time in prison valuable. She finally had time for herself, and she spent her last days reading, reflecting, and praying, quietly awaiting the inevitable death sentence she knew she was about to receive.

Trial and Sentence

Less than two months after her arrest and confession, Edith Cavell and the other hosts from the underground refugee network (35 men and women) stood in front of the German military tribunal in the Belgian Senate Chamber. Determined not to bring the nursing profession into disgrace, Cavell appeared in civil clothes. When accused of leading soldiers to Germany's enemies, she claimed that her intent was not to help the enemy but to aid those seeking to reach the Dutch border. The trial was brief, and the accused were not allowed legal representation. After two days of deliberation, General von Sauberzweig, the German Military Governor of Brussels, decided their fate. Blinded by bitterness because his son had been gravely injured fighting British soldiers, the general showed no mercy in deciding. Edith and six other hosts received the death sentence. The others were to spend many years in prison. By this time, the outrage of their arrest and trial spurred diplomatic moves from several neutral countries, including The Netherlands, Spain, and the United States. But their plea for clemency came far too late for Edith Cavell and one of her companions. General von Sauberzweig wouldn't hear their pleas and, wanting to get what he considered a nuisance over with, ordered the prompt execution of those who received the death sentence. None of the diplomats pleading for clemency had the power to contradict him, and they'd run out of time. The execution date was set for the next day.

Learning Her Fate and Execution

Nurse Cavell received the news of having only a few hours to live with the same stoic calm with which she had conducted her care and escape network operation. Talking to the chaplain on her last night alive, she revealed that after working with people so close to death throughout her life, she wasn't afraid of dying. She expressed her gratitude for the time she had to reflect on her past and the kindness of the people who surrounded her during her last days. She didn't regret that her patriotic spirit led to her death. She was happy to have helped the wounded and those seeking freedom. She also said that she didn't resent the Germans or the informants who had ultimately betrayed her. Her last wish was not to be remembered as a martyr but as a nurse who did her duty of saving lives in good faith and without discrimination. The following morning, she completed her diary by documenting the date of her death as October 12, 1915.

Passing German soldiers who stood with their heads bowed, unable to look the brave and beautifully dressed woman walking in front of them in the eye, Edith Cavell and her friend and colleague Philippe Baucq were led from their Saint Gilles prison cells across Brussels to the Belgian National Firing Range. As they faced the German firing squad, their sentences were read aloud amid the weeping cries of the outraged public (including Cavell's nursing companions). Tears filled Cavell's eyes before they were bandaged, but she walked valiantly to the execution post, where she died immediately after receiving the shots.

The Aftermath

General von Sauberzweigs's hopes to put the issue of Edith Cavell behind him by a swift execution were short-lived. By dying in front of the German firing squad for aiding her compatriots (and despite her wishes to be remembered as a nurse), Edith Cavell became a martyr. To the eyes of the world, the Germans executed a heroine, news that was received with widespread condemnation.

The main reason for the intense condemnation was the extensive press coverage of Cavell's arrest and the selfless acts she had performed. Even German writers spoke highly of her, like Dr. Benn, a German chief medical officer who asked to witness Cavell's trial and execution. He remarked that beyond being ordered to attend, he became invested in following the trial after speaking to Nurse Cavell. He found her an exceptionally brave woman, worthy of the title of heroine with which Britain was to honor her after her death. As Dr. Benn described, Edith Cavell met her death with a demeanor only those who are at peace with themselves have. Still, as a German, the doctor agreed with her punishment since she committed a serious crime under German military law. It also fell upon him to verify her death and place her body in a coffin, after which she was immediately buried right there, at the rifle range. A simple wooden cross was used to mark her grave (parts of this cross were later transported with her body to Norfolk and preserved in the church of her hometown).

General von Sauberzweig's miscalculation cost him and the German military dearly. While not being able to save her, the American embassy made sure the news of Edith Cavell's execution became as widespread as possible. As the press picked up the story, the Germans realized their mistake. While they were used to making quick military decisions (especially in wartime) and didn't think the death of a nurse would cause an outcry, they didn't calculate her death being used as propaganda against them. Using Cavell's martyrdom and unjust death (preceded by a trial without legal representation), the Allied countries could present the Germans as veritable monsters. While this was contrary to her wishes, it was a great way to ensure that Cavell's incredibly courageous acts aiding those in need would never be forgotten.

Some argue that Cavell's execution played an enormous role in the United States abandoning its neutral position and joining the war against Germany. Whether this is true or not, the event helped sway opinions in Cavell's home country. For eight consecutive weeks after her death, the number of British countrymen responding to army recruitment programs doubled.

While the Germans realized too late that their general had caused irreparable damage to their reputation (and possibly harmed their advancements in the war), they declared that no other women would be executed without a thorough investigation by the Kaiser himself. They also agreed to uphold the clemency pleas submitted on behalf of Louise Thuliez, Countess Jeanne de Belleville, and Louis Severin, the other refuge hosts sentenced to death.

When the Great War ended, Edith Cavell posthumously received the "Cross of the Order of Leopold" from King Albert I of Belgium, the "Croix Civique" from the Belgian government, and the "Légion d'Honneur" award from the French government.

Edith Cavell's Return Home

On March 17, 1919, Edith Cavell's body was exhumed from her grave at the shooting range, and two months later, her body was transferred to the Gare du Nord in Brussels on a military carriage. On her last voyage in Belgium, Cavell was escorted by a detachment of British troops sent from Cologne, flanked by the masses who wished to express their admiration for the heroine and say their final goodbyes. After a brief service held in her honor at the Gare du Nord, Cavell's coffin was transported to the port of Ostend. From there, it was loaded onto the HMS Rowena, the Royal Navy ship that took it across the English Channel to the Dover port. Several British officers guarded the coffin during the entire voyage.

Upon her body's arrival in Dover, the St Mary's Society of Change Ringers honored Edith Cavell by consecutively ringing for 3 hours and 3 minutes. Her coffin was placed in a reinforced funeral carriage and guarded at Dover overnight for security reasons before being transported to London the next day during daylight hours. Everyone recognized its significance as the train carrying Nurse Cavell's remains was arriving at Victoria Station. As the train passed them, the men tending their fields took off their hats in a silent salutation to their brave heroine. When the train arrived in London, it was welcomed by a mass of nurses, who walked in front of the carriage transporting the coffin to Westminster Abbey. They were flanked by soldiers of all ranks and civilians wanting to pay homage. As the press across the globe would remark afterward, Nurse Edith Cavell was paid a tribute rivaling triumphant warriors. Her memorial service at Westminster Abbey was attended by numerous politicians and royalty who wished to show her the respect she deserved. Edith Cavell was laid to rest in Norwich.

Chapter 4: Alvin York: The Sharpshooter from Tennessee

This chapter places the spotlight on Alvin York, one of the finest sharpshooters of the First World War, who is thought to have captured more than 130 German soldiers on his own. However, to truly understand the significance of this heroic act, the chapter starts by outlining York's initial reluctance to fight due to religious beliefs and subsequent transformation on the battlefield.

Alvin York, one of the finest sharpshooters of the First World War.
https://commons.wikimedia.org/wiki/File:Alvin_C._York_1919.jpg

You'll read about Alvin York's tactics during the engagement of Châtel-Chéhéry in the Argonne Forest of France on October 8, 1918. How York, a skilled marksman with vast experience from his hunting days in the Tennessee Mountains, took it upon himself to neutralize the threat.

Alvin York's Humble Background

Born into a family of farmers in the mountains of Pall Mall, Tennessee, in 1887, Alvin Cullum York grew up in a hard-bitten life. His parents struggled financially living in an isolated area and raising 11 children. Like many children in his position, Alvin left school at an early age and worked to bring money home instead. His employment started at his father's blacksmith shop. When his father passed away in 1911, the family was pushed into deep poverty. As the third oldest child and the oldest son, Alvin took on the responsibility of supporting his family by taking on numerous jobs around Pall Mall. One of these jobs was hunting, which enabled him to become a highly skilled marksman. Shooting was something he enjoyed doing in his free time, too, while exploring the Tennessee Mountains and hunting. Other hobbies included gambling and drinking, which earned him notoriety in the neighboring towns. Gambling drunk, he often lost a lot of money, which further added to the strain he felt weighing on him trying to support his family.

While he avoided church during his childhood and early adulthood, participating in one assembly at the Church of Christ in Christian Union in 1914 was enough to change his views and transform his life. Soon, he became a member of this small congregation and was persuaded to adopt the church's moral code, which prohibited violence. He described his new, awakened state as a radical transformation, allowing him to change his life for the better. After fully adopting pacifism, Alvin York rapidly advanced spiritually, eventually becoming his church's second elder. The formerly known rascal became a gentle giant (he had a formidable 200-pound, 6-foot tall fame) who strove for nothing more than to live peacefully and earn enough to support his family.

His Faith Gets Tested

Alvin York's faith was put to a massive test two years after finding it. By this time, World War I had been ongoing for three years, and the tales of the monumental destruction and losses of thousands of lives had reached the United States. Remaining neutral until 1917, the US ultimately joined the war, and drafting for military service began. After hearing about the horrors of the European battlefields, York wanted to avoid partaking in the war, but he had no choice: signing up for the draft was mandatory. Soon, York received the notification for service and was confronted with a moral dilemma. While his patriotic drive (which he claimed to have inherited from his ancestors) pushed him to take his rifle and fight against the Germans, his religion told him otherwise. However, choosing to defy reporting for military service openly would have resulted in his arrest, so he initially tried to get out of it through other means. His first tactic was to simply explain that his religion doesn't allow him to partake in the war. He made his appeal twice and was denied both times. While exceptions for conscientious objections based on religious or moral convictions were upheld by the United States Army, York's church wasn't an officially recognized branch, so his beliefs weren't considered a valid reason not to enter the army. His pastor also pleaded on his behalf but was denied for the same reason.

By late fall of 1971, York had no alternative but to report to his assigned service post, Camp Gordon, Georgia. Serving in the 328th Infantry Regiment, 82nd Infantry Division, York soon gained a reputation for his skilled marksmanship. Still reluctant to fight in a live battle, he made a final plea to his commander, Major Edward Buxton, explaining that fighting would directly contradict his beliefs. As a religious man, Buxton didn't immediately deny York's appeal. Instead, the commander sat the young officer down and encouraged him to discuss his beliefs. Responding to York's objections, Buxton used scriptures that supported his views, which aligned with fighting in a war that had already taken so many lives and threatened to take much more.

After spending hours weighing up both sides of the coin, York was even more confused. He asked his commander for a brief time off to contemplate his decision of whether to fight. He returned home and took to the so-familiar mountains, hoping that spending time there would help him make the right choice. After a few days of reflection and prayer, York concluded that as long as he followed the path aligned with his soul, he would remain a good man in the eyes of God, regardless of where this path took him. While still opposed to the war, fighting for his country aligned with his patriotic values, he returned to his battalion, ready to follow orders and fight if necessary. Shortly after, his division was shipped to the French shores and entered the war.

Entering the Great War

As a member of the 82nd Airborne Paratroopers Division, Alvin York was under the command of Sgt. Bernard J. Early. Arriving in Normandy on June 27, 1918, and being a group of highly skilled soldiers, the division was immediately transferred to the front line. They were deployed to the United States' most extensive military operation during the Great War (as it was known then), the Meuse-Argonne Offensive. York and 16 men from the unit were tasked with seizing two shipments arriving through the railway, an assignment that wouldn't have been easy even had they been given the correct guidance to their destination. However, because York's unit was given a French map, none of the members could read it properly, so they got lost and ended up being cut off behind enemy lines. Here, they came across a small unit of German soldiers. While they easily overpowered the Germans, their troubles had just begun, and the events that followed helped Alvin York enter history as one of the greatest war heroes of American history.

The captured Germans knew they were still on their territory, so they called for backup. The backup that came was none other than a machine-gun battalion, which the Americans couldn't see earlier as it was stationed on the other side of heavy underbrush. The captured Germans' plan to yell until their comrades came to their aid succeeded, and on October 8, 1918, York and his division found themselves under a vicious attack from the German machine guns. Besides marching on and firing their fortified machine guns, the German soldiers also attacked with gas, immediately killing nine members of the American unit. As York described in his diary (where he diligently recorded the war's events), his fellow soldiers went down in the attack like blades of grass before a lawnmower. Since their sergeant was among the fallen, York, who was next in the line of command, took over. He ordered his men to take cover and focus on returning fire as best as they could. This only angered the Germans even more, and they fired on the Americans from every direction. Alvin York remained where he was, and as most of the machine guns were now targeting him, he took them on, one by one.

Using His Hunting Experience

Using his trusty rifle and the skills gained from hunting in the Tennessee Mountains, York slowly worked his way toward the guns. It proved an effective tactic since he was a remarkable shooter. Advancing slowly and calmly, York picked off a German soldier with each shot, making no mistakes. All he had to do was wait until they raised their heads and fire. He knew neither he nor his men would be safe until he took down the machine guns. He calculated that the Germans had about 30 machine guns, so he had a few more to get through.

Despite being outnumbered, the Americans, especially York, surprised the Germans with their blitz attack and ability to shoot with frightening accuracy. However, after a while, the German soldiers realized that only one American soldier was decimating their ranks and that he was working slowly. So, a few Germans returned the attack and, charging forward, attempted to take down York with their fixed bayonets. By this time, York only had half a clip remaining in his rifle, but his pistol was fully loaded and ready to fire. In a lightning-speed move, he flipped out his pistol and shot at the men charging at him. Once again, he didn't miss a single shot. Seeing their men drop in front of their eyes, the rest of the German unit thought that the lone American shooter had backup. After all, how else could he have reached the machine guns and killed the group of soldiers charging at him without getting hit even once? The Germans thought he must have had help eliminating the machine gun and refused to believe he could have done it all by himself.

Thinking they now faced a large American unit and unwilling to lose more men, the Germans surrendered. After surrendering, the German unit's commander ordered their English-speaking major to facilitate the process and followed the Americans back to their lines. As they marched, other German groups, possibly thinking they were surrounded by more Americans, surrendered to York's group. By the time he emerged from the woods and approached the American lines, they had captured so many German soldiers that York feared that his own artillery would open fire on them, mistaking them for a solely German unit preparing a counterattack. Fortunately, this didn't happen. Lieutenant Woods, the soldier who greeted York's returning unit, was astounded by York's achievement as acting commander, especially when he learned that York had done most of the work himself. Woods counted 132 German soldiers, jokingly remarking that York captured a small German army. In an equally lighthearted fashion (which did not reflect his sentiments), York replied that he only took down a few Germans. Based on his accounts and the recollection of the six surviving soldiers from his unit, besides capturing 132, York also killed between 25 and 35 German soldiers, including those operating the machine guns.

Aftermath

Despite documenting everything regarding the event, including his subsequent promotion to sergeant, York never mentioned anything about his heroic act to his family while stationed overseas. He wrote to them frequently and discussed many topics but wasn't willing to boast about his heroics. His family learned of York's actions after reading about the events of the Meuse-Argonne Offensive in the Saturday Evening Post. The publication detailing the courageous manner in which York took down at least 30 German machine guns and virtually single-handedly captured a large group while being outnumbered beyond the enemy line made Alvin York into a national hero.

Later, York was accused of lying about taking down the machine gun battalion by himself. Claiming it impossible to achieve this with only a rifle and a pistol, his accusers argued that Sergeant Early took down at least half of the men, helping York. They said Early was killed much later than York claimed and launched a protest against giving York the accolades he would receive for his achievements. The United States Army opened an investigation but upheld York's version, discrediting his accusers' claims. Upon returning home, York received the nation's Medal of Honor, the Médaille Militaire, the Distinguished Service Cross, and many other decorations for his bravery. He was surrounded by massive public attention, which made him uncomfortable. He likened those seeking an interview with him to predators circling their prey. Instead of enjoying a good hike in the Tennessee Mountains as he planned to after his return, he was pushed into the spotlight he had never sought.

Beyond the publication of his heroic accomplishment in the press, York was honored by the New York Stock Exchange members, who suspended their operations to invite York into their business and carry him around on their shoulders. In May 1919, Congress honored York with a staggering standing ovation. He received many offers for public appearances ranging from lectures to acting. He promptly turned them down, feeling that selling his story through these public appearances would dishonor his military service.

Later Years and Legacy

Instead of taking on the lucrative proposals he was offered, Alvin York returned to his peaceful life in Tennessee. He married and worked on the farm he received from the state (one of the few prizes he accepted besides his medals), along with hunting and blacksmithing. Staying true to his religion, York later dabbled in lay preaching and teaching at a Sunday school.

Slowly accepting that his life would never be as peaceful as he had initially hoped, York embraced the industrial environment he was sucked into. While he rarely talked about the event that had brought him fame, he did use his fame to raise funds for the Jamestown Industrial School named after him. York taught and served as the president of a high school established for mountain children living in rural Tennessee areas. He established the York Agricultural Institute in Jamestown, which sought to educate the youth of his hometown, Pall Mall.

Reporters from across the country, politicians hoping to use York's name in their campaigns, and Hollywood screenwriters wanting to purchase the rights to his story would often visit him. While he welcomed everyone on his farm, he kept turning down the offers until much later, when Hollywood executives finally convinced him to approve of making a movie about his heroic acts.

While he was under the assumption that he could tell not only what happened in France but also what it took for him to get there and everything he had done since returning home, the movie Sergeant York (1941) was based solely on the French battle. World War II was already active when the film was released, which impacted York's story even more, and not only for the public. Military officials were reminded of the deadly capabilities of new technologies, prompting them to find more efficient ways to outdo the enemy. Moreover, his heroic acts inspired many young soldiers to enlist and achieve their own outstanding achievements during World War II.

At the same time, Alvin York experienced another benefit of the Industrial Revolution and wanted to bring this to his hometown. He felt the need to prepare the next generation for what was to come so that people wouldn't feel isolated in rural communities. Growing up in a small community consisting of little more than a few cabins allocated sparsely across the mountains, York didn't have access to much technology or knowledge in his youth. He turned to drinking and gambling because he didn't have much else to do, and he wished to spare the next generation from falling into the same trap.

He used the income and additional recognition he gained from the movie to garner resources for furthering youth education in his community. For example, he won his internal moral battle by letting his core values lead him down a path of selfless sacrifice in the army, and he continued his selfless acts to better others' lives. Spending the rest of his life fearing condemnation in God's eyes for resorting to violence and killing the German soldiers, he strove to give back as much as he could, not letting his war experiences define him. He wanted his legacy to become more than that of a man who single-handedly took down a German unit of heavily reinforced machine guns, and he went on to achieve nationwide celebrity status. However, those who learn his true story understand the significance of his actions in his heroic feat at that one fateful event and his strength to do what he did despite his religious beliefs urging him to do otherwise.

Alvin York died in Nashville, Tennessee, after a long illness. The 76-year-old veteran was laid to rest in Pall Mall while his legacy continues to linger in his beloved hometown and across the nation. Closer to home, he is remembered as a dedicated educator who helped prepare the coming generation for the changes brought on by the Industrial Revolution. Across the United States and beyond, Alvin York is known as a war hero who showed extraordinary courage in facing the enemy.

Chapter 5: Eugene Bullard: The Black Swallow of Death

In addition to facing the horrors of war, Eugene Bullard fought the shackles of racist oppression. Before becoming the first African American fighter pilot in WWI, Bullard had an interesting life navigating the world through oppression. Bullard wore many hats, taking on multiple identities throughout his life. From a boxer, a traveling performer, a pilot, a spy, and a civil rights activist, Bullard sucked all the nectar out of every aspect of existence. His heroism extended beyond the war. Despite facing massive hurdles, his inspiring self-determination is a trait anyone facing adversity should emulate.

Eugene Bullard fought the shackles of racist oppression.
https://commons.wikimedia.org/wiki/File:Eugene_Bullard_in_Legionnaire_Uniform.jpg

Bullard never let others' opinions or the difficulties attached to his skin color hold him back. He fought to overcome personal limitations and prejudices to rise to the top of European society. Bullard's life was crammed with adventures, obstacles, and triumphs. It's a pity that Bullard was not recognized in the United States as the hero he was until after his death, and why keeping the name of this incredible human alive is crucial. The roads Eugene Bullard paved opened the way for the brilliant black talents who followed in his military footsteps and the civil rights struggle.

From his humble beginnings as a farm boy to the upper echelons of French society and rubbing shoulders with celebrities like Picasso and Salvador Dali, Bullard achieved what many black people in his time would consider a distant dream. The color barriers that Bullard kicked down paved the way for numerous activists to rise beyond the chains of racial oppression. Through his many iterations as a warrior, night club owner, street performer, and spy, Bullard always embodied a pride and dignity that would never allow anybody to undermine him for his skin color. He constantly pushed against the prejudiced status quo, paving the way for the African American people who came after him and who would struggle for the right to fulfill their potential.

As one of only a handful of black pilots who flew in WWI, Bullard is included in an elite group that reformed the military. Many white pilots of the era felt that a black man would never achieve what they could behind the controls of an advanced aircraft, so Bullard's military career was a constant uphill battle for recognition. Not only did the multifaceted pilot heroically fight on the front lines of war, but he also fought on the battlefield in the struggle for freedom and equality. Bullard's wild and inspiring life almost sounds like a movie directed by Quentin Tarantino, yet the outrageous events actually happened. Prepare yourself to relive the details of one of the most authentic, resilient, and adventurous lives ever. Bullard's intriguing existence is a testament to what can be achieved with self-belief, bravery, authenticity, and an unfaltering drive to kick down the doors people insist you cannot open.

Early Life

Bullard was born in 1895 in Columbus, Georgia, as the son of formerly enslaved people. The future looked bleak for the young man born in one of the most oppressive places in the world for an African American. From a young age, Bullard understood that he had to escape the tin can town that kept him trapped to fully realize his unlimited potential. As much as Bullard's parents attempted to protect him from the racist realities of living in the South, his delusions would soon be shattered as oppression came knocking at his door. Bullard's father got into a fight with a white supervisor at his workplace, causing a lynch mob to attack his father. They didn't succeed in killing him, but he was severely hurt. Even after this tragic event, Bullard's father instilled in him the importance of carrying himself with dignity despite the popular, horrendous beliefs about the inferiority of black people that permeated the culture at the time.

Following the attempted lynching, Bullard tried to run away from home multiple times. One of his attempts caused his father to give him a terrible beating out of fear of the dangers the young boy could have encountered. However, at age 11, Bullard successfully ran away despite his father's best efforts to prevent it. The trauma of seeing the man he respected and loved dearly forced into such a horrific position permanently shifted Bullard's outlook and perception of the Southern community in which he grew up. At the tender age of 11, he knew that living in Georgia, he would never be treated equal to his white peers, and this reality did not sit well with his ambitious and liberated spirit. He roamed the streets of Georgia for five years, desperately seeking a way out. Eventually, he met a band of English gypsies who sang the praises of a more progressive European society welcoming black people.

Bullard knew he would not manifest his dreams in the United States due to the societal attitudes and institutions that held black people back. By today's standards, European society back then would be considered racist, but they were far ahead of America. Bullard was determined to find any way to leave the oppressive shores of the country he called home in search of greener pastures. He was brave enough to leap into the unknown, starting fresh with no help or family he could call on. However, his charismatic charm, impenetrable spirit, and unbridled ambition built a reality that etched his name into the history books.

Bullard developed a singular focus on getting to Europe even though he did not have any plans for what he would do once he got there. In 1912, as a 16-year-old teenager, Bullard stowed away on a ship headed to Germany. Bullard got off in Scotland, where he immediately noticed how the local population treated him much better than the abuse he was used to receiving in Georgia. Bullard had no idea what he would do on this new foreign continent, but it felt better than what he had experienced at home.

From Scotland, Bullard made his way to England. Bullard's charisma and natural talent enabled him to work numerous odd jobs, including being a street performer, working on a dock, being a target at an amusement park, and even becoming a skilled lightweight and middleweight boxer. Bullard moved on from England and ended up in France, a country he fell in love with. Bullard recounted how France's developed and robust democracy made white and black people from the United States treat one another like brothers. Bullard had arrived in the country where he would build his military name.

Experiences Flying for France

By the time Bullard was 19, he had experienced enough adventures for several lifetimes, but his journey toward excellence was only just beginning. He joined the legendary French Foreign Legion to fight Germany in the war. He was transferred to another unit, where he got wounded trying to deliver a message to another French officer. His injuries prevented him from ever successfully participating in ground combat again. However, he was awarded for his bravery with an awesome nickname, "The Black Swallow of Death," and the Croix de Guerre military decoration.

While recovering from his wounds in a clinic in Lyon, he met a French air service officer. The officer grew fond of Bullard and offered to help him become a gunman in a French aircraft. In 1916, Bullard trained as an aircraft gunner in Bordeaux. During his training, Bullard learned about the La Fayette Escadrille, a group of Americans flying under the French banner. Knowing there might be a chance to join his countrymen in air combat, he obtained a pilot's license. The prestigious team earned a lot of money and was highly respected among the French ranks, enticing Bullard into applying himself. In seven months, Bullard achieved his goal of becoming a certified pilot. He partied late into the night in the French capital of Paris. He shouted from the rooftops excitedly, alerting every American in the city that he had achieved the seemingly impossible.

In November 1917, Bullard shot two aircraft out of the sky using the Fokker Triplane and a Pfalz D.III. It was a significant milestone for the pilot who had ambitions to fly for his country of origin someday. This dream was within reach as the opportunity emerged to join the La

Fayette Escadrille with the US Air Force when America entered the war. However, his eagerness was not enough to convince some of his racist superiors. Some officers even campaigned to have him removed from the air service.

Racial Challenges

Bullard's talents were overlooked by his countrymen. When he initially earned his pilot's license, the media did not publish a word about his incredible story, most likely due to racial prejudices. The only magazine to print a story about Bullard was the NAACP-run "The Crisis," which mentioned his enlistment into the Air Service but did not go into much depth. Whether it was governmental censorship or self-imposed silence, the racist American media was not yet willing to acknowledge the achievements of an African American war hero. The United States society was structured so no African American achievements could be recognized or promoted. Bullard's accomplishments would be undermined by his countrymen at every step of his journey, so he embraced France more than America as his home.

Bullard was hit with one of the biggest racist blows of his military career when the American Air Force rejected his application to join. Despite having flown 20 combat missions and having two unconfirmed kills, Bullard's entry into the service was denied. The official reason was that he was required to hold the rank of First Lieutenant before joining. However, the most likely motivation for the rejection of the skilled pilot was the racial biases that existed in the U.S. military. As much as Bullard praised the enlightened French society, he got into a racially motivated dispute with a French officer upon his return to the Aéronautique Militaire. This dispute resulted in his being transferred to a different regiment, where he ended his military career after being discharged in 1919.

The attitude of white American soldiers that entered the war was demoralizing. Many top-ranking leaders within the armed forces believed that if white soldiers saw black fighters living freely and unsegregated, it would demotivate the American troops. What was especially concerning for some fighters who held racist sentiments was that they would have to see black soldiers mixing with white women. Many black soldiers were defamed by racists in the military. Black troops were unjustly accused of being cowards or of committing even more despicable acts like sexual assault. Racism blinded many American soldiers to the great servicemen the black warriors were. They could not look past skin color and recognize the tremendous character and courage their black counterparts exhibited on and off the battlefield. Their prejudices were so profoundly instilled that they failed to see what was right in front of them.

The Linard memo was the most transparent document depicting the extent of American racism. The memo, addressed to the French military and civilian authority figures, outlined how, in the United States, black people were seen as inferior. The memo continued explaining that strong bonds should not be formed between white and black officers in the French military. The memo described that they could not accept black soldiers flying with white Americans because it would deeply upset them and possibly impact their effectiveness in battle. Thankfully, the French government denounced the horrifically prejudiced letter and refused to acknowledge it as justified. The Americans constantly pushed to inflict their racial paradigm on French society within the military. The experiences black soldiers had abroad helped them reframe how they thought about themselves and sparked the flames of racial justice when they returned to the oppressive United States.

No matter where Bullard went, he was always fighting an uphill battle against racism. Regardless of how much he proved himself, there were always people who saw him as inferior. This burden weighed heavy on his shoulders because, since childhood, he wanted to flee from discrimination based on skin color. His desire to end racial oppression led him to become a civil rights activist standing up for the dignity and self-determination of all African Americans. As much as Bullard wanted to be seen as equal, the racial dynamics of the time never allowed him to escape the discriminatory attitudes of ignorant bigots.

Bullard's battle with racism would not end when the war did. Upon his return to America, he had to face many discriminatory battles that led him to return to France because the treatment toward him had become unbearable. His love for his country was counteracted by the misery inflicted on him by its citizens. The tumultuous relationship he had with his home country would plague him for his entire life because he could not rise to the top of American society, even as a war hero. The infinite barriers before him were enough to break this resilient man so much that he could not stand to spend another second in the United States. The tragic past of racial abuse prevented the government and civil society from bestowing upon Bullard the credit he deserved during his lifetime.

The Symbolism of His Plane's Emblem

As an entertainer, Bullard was somewhat of an eccentric. In addition to flying with his rhesus monkey mascot, Jimmy, he had a heart pierced by a dagger insignia on his Spad 7C.1 plane. Underneath the heart was the slogan "All blood runs red." Traditionally, a heart with a dagger plunged through it represented pain or sacrifice. The symbol combining violence with love is perfectly suited for a military man because he fights for the love of his country or his ideals. The slogan highlighted Bullard's belief in equality because regardless of skin color, everybody bleeds red. The slogan has some pain attached to it in the context of war because it shows that every person in combat will bleed. Not everybody was permitted to paint their planes, so it was a great privilege for Bullard to fly this insignia with pride.

Post-War Experiences

After the First World War, Bullard's life did not get any less intriguing. Instead of retiring to the quiet countryside to relax after his years of service, he opted to stay in the middle of various actions. He never returned to America when the war ended since he had been treated more fairly in French society and saw an opportunity to excel. Due to his military decoration, Bullard earned French citizenship. He built a successful life in the country after the war and would continue serving the nation into the Second World War and beyond.

Bullard gravitated toward Paris' nightlife, working in a nightclub called Zelli's. He owned the Le Grand Duc nightclub and L'Escadrille, an American-themed bar. In this era, Bullard befriended many famous and influential people. On the list of celebrities he knew was F. Scott Fitzgerald, author of the classic novel "The Great Gatsby," and the revolutionary and controversial performer Josephine Baker. The Jazz scene in Paris was thriving, and as a man who loved a great party, Bullard took full advantage monetarily and socially. His activeness in the scene allowed him to meet many celebrities, becoming close friends with many. Josephine Baker, who made as many strides for civil rights as Bullard did, babysat for him on multiple occasions.

Just like Josephine Baker in the lead-up to WWII, Bullard took on the role of a spy. He was recruited to listen to French Nazi supporters in his bars and report their discussions to the relevant authorities. Once the

Second World War had begun, Bullard reenlisted in the 51st Infantry Regiment, where he was devastatingly injured in a terrible explosion. He was no longer fit to fight and had to flee France to avoid Nazi capture. He took the arduous journey through Spain into Portugal and back to the United States, the country he had left all those years ago. But, instead of heading back to the South, he ended up in the bastion of African American culture, Harlem, New York.

Far from the glitz and glamor of his Parisian lifestyle, Bullard worked as a security guard and longshoreman in New York. Bullard was involved in an altercation with a racist mob and police officers in 1949 while attending a Paul Robeson concert. He was beaten by police, prompting him to take up the civil rights cause as an activist. He experienced another racially motivated incident because, in rebellion against the oppressive attitudes of society, he refused to sit in the back of the bus as expected of black people. Fatigued by the constant battle to merely exist as a black man in America, Bullard returned to France, where he was received as a hero.

The more progressive France gave the military hero a lofty honor by making him a knight of the Legion of Honor in 1959, a decoration reserved for the highest military achievement. Before this award, in 1954, he was chosen as part of an elite group to relight the eternal flame at the Tomb of the Unknown Soldier. He shared this privilege with only two other men. The tragedy of Bullard's life is that as much as he loved the United States, the racist society did not love him back. Luckily, he found a home in Paris where he was given the respect and accolades he deserved. Bullard was a multidimensional character who expressed his greatness in several ways. Thirty-three years after his death, America finally recognized his contributions to the First and Second World Wars. The United States Air Force posthumously appointed him as a second lieutenant. In 2019, Bullard was immortalized in a statue at the Museum of Aviation in his home state of Georgia. The new enlightened America could finally celebrate one of its greatest heroes.

Chapter 6: Captain Noel Godfrey Chavasse: From the Olympics to Battlefield Healer

Noel Godfrey Chavasse was the quintessential gentleman of his time. He was an upper-middle-class academic who excelled in intellectual circles and sports. Chavasses represented Britain in the 1908 Olympics for the 400m sprint. Not only did he make it into the highest level of competition in athletics, but he also became a passionate and respected medical doctor. His intellectual prowess and superior physical fitness were the perfect combination for creating a brave war hero.

Captain Noel Godfrey Chavasse.
https://www.flickr.com/photos/imperialwarmuseum/9367593625

Letters from the battlefield that history has stored reflect the realities of war, from optimism to the dire times of an uncertain future. Through his battles and dark times, Chavasse rose as one of the most decorated soldiers in the war and a symbol of resilience and healing as a key member of the Royal Army Medical Corps. Chavasse met a horrific demise amid a shelling battle, leaving the brave soldier unrecognizable. His bravery and sacrifice are memorialized with a statue in Abrocmby Square, highlighting the necessity of doctors on the battlefield.

Chavasse was a man of faith and virtue. His Christian background and compassionate nature allowed him to put others before himself, eventually costing him his life. Having been raised in the church, Chavasse saw his mission as higher than the physical plane. His courage and the care for the men he displayed in the trenches cannot be described as anything short of divine. Although he experienced his own mental and physical hardships, he swept them to the side to serve his brother in arms. Not many are made of the same indescribable material as Captain Noel Godfrey Chavasse, which is why it is crucial to ensure that his name gets echoed through the ages as an inspiration for what it means to unselfishly serve your community.

Childhood Days

Captain Chavasse was born in Oxford in 1884. Chavasse was one of seven children and had an identical twin brother. His father was a reverend, so Chavasse grew up in a religious household that deeply instilled Christian values of unselfishness, humility, and fighting for what was right. This may have significantly influenced Chevasse's heroic actions later in life. Chevasse's father, Rev. Francis Chavasse, was the Lord Bishop of Liverpool and was highly respected throughout the country. His father would also found the prestigious St. Peter's College in Oxford.

Chavasse's extraordinary athletic ability was cultivated in his school days. He attended Magdalen College School and later enrolled in Liverpool College before finally finishing his formal education at Trinity College. In university, Chavasse earned his *blue status* (colors given to students who compete at the highest level of sporting competition). Chavasse was a lacrosse Blue in the season of 1905 to 1906 and was an athletics blue for both the 100-yard and 440-yard dash. Both Chavasse and his twin Christopher competed in the 1908 Olympics.

Since childhood, Chevasse dreamed of achieving glory for defending his country – and practically mapped out his way to becoming the only person to be awarded two Victoria crosses in the First World War. The 16-year-old Chavasse kept a scrapbook called "Snow Flakes," which contained elaborate drawings of medieval knights and fictitious stories of righteous soldiers emerging victorious out of exciting battles. The scrapbook was rediscovered after 119 years and gives a snapshot into the idealistic mind of a young Chavasses who would slowly become tainted by the terrors of war before he met his tragic end. The scrapbook also contained images and descriptions of historic battles like Waterloo. It is clear from early on that Chavasse was meant to play an instrumental role in reshaping the world through the tragedies of warfare.

The education that resulted from Chavsse's relatively privileged upbringing and the religious values instilled by his reverend father shaped Chevasse into a well-rounded man who stretched himself into multiple spheres of life. His intriguing writing and the watercolor artistry displayed in his teenage scrapbook show how Chevasse explored multiple aspects of life through which to filter his chivalrous ideology influenced by his culture, time, and upbringing.

Chevasse's dreams were common for young men in his position, but he had the drive and courage to manifest them through unbridled ambition and an unstoppable work ethic. His dedication to intellect, creativity, morality, and the bravery to fight for his beliefs using his gift of healing created fertile soil to plant the seeds of heroism. His upbringing and English education prepared him for the nationalistic pride and moral compass to put himself before others as a young man laying his life down for his country and fellow servicemen. The dreams of glory he had as a child would come to pass, but unfortunately, he would be listed among the heroes who gave their lives in battle, not surviving to tell the tales of his contributions to WWI victory.

With the medical profession, Chavasse found an avenue to be helpful in the war effort while promoting his selfless and humble nature to serve his fellow soldiers on the battlefield. Unlike many war heroes who are awarded for the bodies they leave lying behind, Chevasse reached the peak of the military with his ability to heal others in the worst conditions while disregarding his life and safety. It seems Chevasse was able to predict his tragic fate in the tales of war he recorded in his childhood scrapbook. The pristine watercolor paintings of his beloved Liverpool and the violent gore of fictional and historical accounts highlighted the paradox of Chavasse, the soldier who healed instead of harming.

Moral Character

His religious Anglican upbringing greatly influenced Chavasse's upright moral character and humility. The Captain kept his faith until he died. His unexplainable commitment to ensuring the men around him were safe and treated was likely due to his adherence to the Christian faith taught him by his father, whom he loved dearly. Chevasse was a devout practitioner of his religion and held conservative views on many aspects of life, including family and promiscuity. Chevasse promoted clean living, which may have contributed to his outstanding physical condition. He never partook in alcohol and lived a healthy lifestyle by eating well and regularly exercising.

During his time in college, Chavasse's optimism shone through strongly. He often wrote to his family about religion and his sporting achievements. Once Chavasse entered the war effort in the Royal Army Medical Corps, letters he wrote back home, mostly to his father, grew darker in tone. He wrote about his fellow soldiers who had lost their lives and the difficulties of maintaining morale and hygiene in their camps. He also wrote about how soldiers were overworked and described how, regardless of his injuries, he was dedicated to searching the battlefield for soldiers who were wounded and needed care. Finances also became a concern for Chavasse, who lamented how he would not have enough money to care for his family when he returned from war. His faith and sense of duty kept him pushing forward in these difficult times until he met his tragic end.

Chavasse's faith and strong moral character fueled his drive to help injured soldiers. Despite suffering himself on the doorstep of death, he suppressed his pain and agony in the service of others, eventually losing his life because of it. Self-sacrifice was a huge part of his faith, as Chavasse was a devout Christian who believed that Christ had given his life for him. Therefore, he embodied the spirit of his Savior by putting himself in harm's way for the benefit of others. His selflessness is why he was awarded two Victoria Crosses, one of which he received after his death. Captain Noel Godfrey Chavasse stands tall as a symbol of unity, brotherhood, and commitment to your team in the most dire circumstances. He not only embodied the attitude of a perfect soldier but showcased a moral character that is almost beyond comprehension, considering how self-centered most people are.

The Captain understood that without virtue and an ideological grounding, being sent into the war meant being a "flanneled fool" or a "muddied oaf," as he called it. Chavasse was propelled by his understanding of the Bible as interpreted by the Anglican background that his father had instilled in him since he was a little boy. Chavasse formulated what it meant to be an ethical soldier with a purpose through the lens of divine inspiration. In his letters that history has preserved, Chavasse's perception of the soldiers lost in battle showed deep compassion and empathy. He never wrote of them as numbers of the frontlines, but he saw them as individuals, so the losses greatly disturbed and saddened him. In one letter, Chavasse writes to the mother of a wounded soldier, describing how she may not be hearing from him because he is bedridden. Instead of writing mechanically, he had enough compassion to go into detail about her son's condition while showing empathy and restraint in the face of a mother potentially losing a son.

The memorial service held after his death was indicative of his faith and piety. They sang his favorite hymns and spoke about his devotion to his God and the church. One of the accounts of his expression of faith in the middle of the war was recorded in a letter to his father. Chavsse described receiving holy communion in a dilapidated church. He wrote of how moving it was to see men kneeling before the Lord to receive the sacrament, further outlining that this was the highest expression of masculinity that he had perceived during his time in war. Chavasse's faith was central to his life, and all the achievements that he had amassed stemmed from his adherence to his religious beliefs and the profound connection he felt with his God.

Early Career

Noel Chavasse graduated from the world-famous Oxford University in 1912. He studied medicine and was awarded the Derby Exhibition, the school's top medical prize. A year later, he joined the Royal Army Medical Corps. While studying, Chavasse was a competitive athlete, making it to the Olympics. Chavasse never won a medal and finished third in his heat, which meant he could not progress to the semi-finals because only the winners of each heat went forward. However, this athletic skill would later help him in his military career. Being able to carry people over long distances and perform incredible endurance tasks is part of what separates him from the average soldier. His physical prowess and empathy resulted in him moving up the ranks to Captain and eventually earning more decorations than any other British soldier in WWI.

In 1910, Chavasse joined the Oxford University Officers' Training Corps medical unit before becoming a Fellow of the Royal College of Surgeons after some additional specialist training. Everything seemed to go amazingly, so he joined the Royal Army Medical Corps. However, the war commenced shortly after he signed up. Chavasse was a lieutenant surgeon for the 10th battalion of the King's Liverpool Regiment, more colloquially known as the Liverpool Scottish. The legendary battalion became one of the most famous after the war, in large part due to the courageous feats of Chavasse.

Chavasse was eventually promoted to Captain due to the valor he displayed on the battlefield. The first military decoration he received was a Military Cross in 1915 for his valiant bravery at the battle of Hooge in Belgium. In this battle, his battalion was introduced to the flamethrower, one of the most terrifying weapons of the First World War. The carnage and devastation were unimaginable. Chavasse went into the disputed ground to rescue wounded soldiers. He tirelessly endured for two days straight, not stopping until he was sure that all the wounded men were retrieved and treated. Although the battle at Hooge was terrifying, Chavasse would encounter exponentially greater carnage as his military career progressed, but he still showed the same bravery, eventually giving his life for his cause.

Most Decorated British Soldier of WWI

Many bravely gave their lives in the trenches of WWI, but few have reached the honors that Chavasse was able to achieve. The Captain was rare amongst the rare, having been awarded two Victoria Crosses, an honor that he shares with only two other soldiers. He earned his first Victoria Cross shortly after the battle at Hooge on August 9. His battalion launched a full frontal assault in the German trenches, but the results were disastrous. A lack of planning and adequate strategy resulted in hundreds of soldiers losing their lives to German weapons within only a few hours. Chavasse exposed himself to enemy fire, exhibiting the same sense of duty he had at Hooge earlier in the year.

Under the cover of darkness, Chavasse went as close as 25 yards to the German trenches in no man's land. Accompanied by a stretcher-bearer, he searched every corner of the battlefield, sometimes under intense fire, to save wounded soldiers. Even when he got injured himself, he continued out of determination and virtue. He managed to save the lives of at least 20 critically injured soldiers and many others who had wounds that were not life-threatening. He continued returning to the battlefield over two days and even carried one soldier across 500 yards under heavy fire. Despite the horrors that he experienced, he kept a positive attitude to keep his team's morale up. His medical knowledge, bravery, and resilience are what made him the perfect candidate for the coveted Victoria Cross award.

As a leader and a medic, Chavasse was concerned with physical and mental health, which was way ahead of his time. In the trenches of WWI, men would often have nervous breakdowns, being unable to cope with the constant strain of battle. Chavasse closely observed his men, and when the fighting got too much for some of the soldiers, he would send them to a low-pressure region so that they could have some time to recover. This was an uncommon practice at the time, as mental health science had hardly progressed at all. Chavasse used his compassion as a guide to his decision-making and empathetically connected with distressed men under his command.

Unfortunately, his second Victoria Cross could not be received while he was living. After his battalion got posted at Wieltje, near Ypres, they attempted to retake Passchendaele Ridge from the Germans. The precision of the German artillery and the devastating use of mustard gas left 143 men dead, including two officers. On the first day of battle, Chavasse was horrendously wounded with a shot to the skull. He was commanded to leave so that he could recover, but he refused for the benefit of his men. He continued to seek out wounded men in the field until he could no longer continue out of sheer exhaustion. After only two days of rest, he returned to no man's land to seek out more wounded soldiers and was directly hit by a German shell. Even though his injuries were dire, he crawled for half a mile to seek out more critically injured troops. He was no longer in the condition to refuse being evacuated, but it was too late. He succumbed to his injuries in a hospital bed and was awarded another Victoria Cross for his courage in extreme adversity. At the end of his life, he was disfigured beyond recognition.

Chavasse was so committed to his men that, against common sense, he chose to stay and serve despite his extreme injuries. Often, war heroes are remembered for their kills, but Chavasse is memorialized for the men whom he gave his life to heal and keep safe from mental and physical injury. He had no regard for his own wounds but laid his life down so that his fellow soldiers could return safely to their families. His courage, faith, and virtuous nature could not allow him to leave his men stranded in no man's land. Even to his dying breath, he was insistent on doing what was best for his men, disregarding what was best for him.

Commemoration

Chavasse's impeccable character and unreplicable valor make him one of the most memorialized soldiers of WWI. He has two headstones representing his Victoria Crosses at his Brandhoek New Military Cemetary grave. Chavasse's medals were purchased at a world record price of £1.5 million and are now displayed at the Imperial War Museum. Chavasse Park in Liverpool is named after the auspicious family. His brother Christopher later became the Bishop of Rochester due to his deep religious study and piety, most likely inspired by their clerical father.

Memorial to Noel Chavasse at the Holy Family Church, Brandhoek.
Wernervc, CC BY-SA 3.0 <https://creativecommons.org/licenses/by-sa/3.0>, via Wikimedia Commons https://commons.wikimedia.org/wiki/File:Noel_Chavasse_-2.jpg

Chavasse's medical dedication has also not been forgotten. A ward at the Walton Centre in Liverpool has been named after him to honor the memory of his selfless adherence to making sure those who needed it would be helped even at the detriment of himself. In Oxford, two paving stones represent his Victoria Crosses near the schools he attended, namely, St. Peter's College and Magdalen College School. A statue of Noel Chavasse tending to soldiers is also displayed at the Army Medical Services Museum. Tom Murphy sculpted a bronze memorial in Abercromby Square for Chavasse and 15 other native Liverpool Victoria Cross holders. In 2017, Chavasse was placed on a £5 commemorative coin minted in both silver and gold as a memorial to mark a century after the First World War.

WWI is considered the first modern war and redefined much of how the world operated. The Great War ushered in the era of nation-states and saw the collapse of the Age of Empires. This transition was later solidified by the end of the WWII. Considering the instrumental role that the British played in the First World War, Chavasse is one of the few men who sat at the forefront of the globe-shifting conflict. Surprisingly, it was not his skills with weapons but rather his courage to save others that propelled him to be one of the heroes of WWI. Therefore, Chavasse stands as a symbol of leading the world not with violence but rather with compassion and a drive to mend what is broken.

Chapter 7: Henry Johnson: The Harlem Hellfighter's Battle

In the accounts of history, the Great War is a pivotal chapter, marked by the valor and sacrifices of countless patriots. This chapter highlights the overlooked story of an unsung hero from that era, weaving a narrative transcending conventional historical accounts. The actions of Henry Johnson, a Harlem Hellfighter, in a singular battle, defined how an indomitable spirit, unmatched bravery, and empathy empowered him to face overwhelming odds during one of history's most tumultuous periods.

Henry Johnson is often overlooked.

https://commons.wikimedia.org/wiki/File:Sergeant_Henry_L_Johnson_American_Soldier_World_War_I.jpg

---

Henry Johnson's undeterred courage and impactful actions in this battle etched his name into the chronicles of heroism. This chapter dissects the circumstances surrounding Johnson's fierce defense of his post against a formidable German force, unraveling the layers of adversity, heroic actions, injuries, and the recognition that transformed him into a symbol of inspiration for many.

The Odds

Before exploring the events during the battle and comprehending the magnitude of Johnson's heroism, it's necessary to grasp the magnitude of the odds stacked against Johnson. The Western Front at that time was the hub of relentless conflict, setting the stage for Johnson's ordeal.

His unit, the Harlem Hellfighters, faced a larger, better-equipped German force. The trenches where the clash unfolded were rife with the echoes of gunfire, the foul scent of mustard gas, and the perpetual fear of imminent assault. The odds seemed insurmountable, yet within this confined position, Johnson stood his ground, confronting the encroaching enemy with unwavering determination.

In the maelstrom of battle, Henry Johnson's actions transcended the ordinary and catapulted him into the realm of legend. Johnson displayed remarkable and unparalleled courage as the German forces bore down on his position. Engaging in hand-to-hand combat, he repelled the enemy with a ferocity that defied the chaos surrounding him. Henry used his gun as a club and a knife to fight against the enemy when he ran out of ammunition. His will to survive and the unwavering determination to defend went beyond the call of duty. Johnson's heroism was not a mere defense of territory but a clear manifestation of the Harlem Hellfighters' creed: an unwavering commitment to duty, honor, and brotherhood.

Although Henry fought relentlessly, warding off the enemy and keeping the victory flag high, avoiding the toll of battle was inevitable. Throughout the intense engagement, he suffered grievous injuries at the hands of the enemy. The wounds inflicted upon him were not only physical but also symbolic of the sacrifices made in the crucible of war. It was reported that Henry Johnson received 21 wounds during the battle, killing four enemy soldiers and injuring more than a dozen, making them retreat. Johnson's body, marked by scars and wounds, bore witness to the price paid for confronting overwhelming odds with unyielding courage.

Subsequent Recognition

Despite the challenges and the personal cost, Henry Johnson's courage did not go unnoticed. His remarkable deeds earned him recognition on the battlefield and in broader circles of society. Johnson's story became a rallying cry for justice and equality, and he emerged as an inspiration for a nation grappling with the aftermath of war.

The further you go into the details of Henry Johnson's battle, you understand that his heroic acts stemmed from his enduring qualities of grit, resilience, and unparalleled courage that made Henry shine even in the darkest of times.

Early Life Struggles

Henry Johnson's early life was surrounded by the racial complexities of the American South during the late 19th and early 20th centuries. Born on July 15, 1892, in Winston-Salem, North Carolina, Johnson entered a world imploding with racial segregation, systemic racism, and deeply ingrained prejudices. At the time, laws enforced strict racial segregation, limiting the path to opportunities and progress for African Americans like Johnson.

Growing up in this challenging environment, Johnson had no choice but to face the harsh realities of discrimination and inequality that were freely practiced and promoted. As educational and economic opportunities were constrained, the promise of a better life seemed far-fetched for many African Americans. In his early days of struggle, he worked various jobs, including as a soda mixer, a chauffeur, a laborer, and a porter at Union Station, Albany. Against these problems, Henry Johnson's decision to enlist in the military reflected personal aspirations and a desire to challenge the limitations imposed by racism.

When World War I started in July 1914, every country, including the US, prepared recruits to defend their homeland. The war allowed Johnson to break free from racial segregation and play his part in the struggle for freedom and democracy. Johnson joined the army, motivated by a sense of duty and a desire for equality.

He enlisted on June 5, 1917, as a private to the 15th New York Regiment, consisting mainly of African Americans and a few white officers. The unit was deployed to France and later renamed the 369th

Infantry Regiment of the 93rd Infantry Division.

The 369th Infantry Regiment, primarily comprised of African American soldiers, later became the Harlem Hellfighters. This unit would distinguish itself on the battlefield, challenging stereotypes and prejudices about the capabilities of black soldiers. For Johnson, enlisting in the Harlem Hellfighters was not merely a military commitment; it was a bold step toward asserting his humanity and challenging the systemic racism that plagued American society.

In the military, there was institutional racism in which African American soldiers were labeled as inferior, low in war capabilities, and were not given the same perks or ranks as their counterparts. The 369th Infantry Regiment faced the dangers of the European front and the challenges of racial discrimination within the military hierarchy. Despite facing systemic obstacles, Johnson and his fellow soldiers sought to prove their worth and patriotism through their actions on the battlefield.

This racial backdrop and Johnson's determination to challenge the prejudices that fueled him forged his character. His enlistment was a personal choice and a deliberate act of defiance against a society that sought to deny him equal rights and recognition.

Preparedness and Training

Besides Henry Johnson's mental capabilities that motivated him to leave a mark, his basic training made him a formidable combatant within the Harlem Hellfighters. He trained in the U.S. Army after his enlistment, learning the foundational elements necessary for a soldier. The training was focused on military discipline, marksmanship, combat basics, and tactical maneuvers. The entire regimen underwent resistance training and physically challenging exercises to meet the demands of warfare on the European front. These exercises included endurance drills, navigating obstacle courses, and long-distance marching. Strength and stamina exercises were equally assigned so the soldier's body could engage and survive in harsh warfare conditions. The training included sessions on improving firearms, sidearms, and grenades so the weapons could be effectively used against the enemy.

After arriving in France, the commanding officers from the U.S. Army assigned the infantry regiment non-combat roles, like unloading supplies, digging trenches, and war-related manual labor. In a turn of events, Maj. Gen. John J. Pershing decided to detach the 369th infantry from other U.S. units to serve with the French Army on April 8, 1918. While the U.S. comrades treated the 369th infantry poorly, the French treated them well. The regiment was taught basic communication phrases in French to communicate with their French comrades.

As the battlefront was crowded with trenches, the soldiers had to learn trench warfare tactics, at which Johnson excelled. The entire regimen trained for days, learning about navigation through the trenches, mastering defensive strategies, and engaging coordinated offensives. This training equipped Johnson with a particular skill set, empowering him to confront challenges posed by trench warfare's dynamic and dangerous landscape.

Lastly, the soldiers' mental toughness was improved in training to prime them to handle the physiological toll of war and make the right decisions during combat. The training included using combat stressors to increase resilience, develop a focused mind, and stay disciplined despite adversity. Maintaining composure and making split-second decisions amid chaos became the hallmark of the mental conditioning that accompanied their military training.

Notably, the bonds formed during training created a cohesive unit, emphasizing trust and cooperation among soldiers. This interconnectedness supported them during tough times, where the reliance on one another became a cornerstone of the collective strength of the Harlem Hellfighters. During his time in military training, Henry Johnson emerged as a physically adept and mentally resilient soldier and a testament to the collective preparedness of the Harlem Hellfighters.

The Nighttime Raid

The Nighttime Raid was the most prominent event in which Johnson made his mark. The Famous Nighttime raid began on the eve of May 14, 1918. The Harlem Hellfighters were posted at the Western Front and encountered skirmishes and gunfire from the enemy for quite some time.

In the shadowed confines of the Western Front trenches during World War I, Henry Johnson's strategic brilliance and resourcefulness took center stage during a fateful nighttime raid on May 14-15, 1918. As darkness draped the battlefield, the Harlem Hellfighters found themselves in a dangerous situation, facing overwhelming odds against a determined German raiding party. As a sentry alongside Needham

Roberts, Johnson demonstrated exceptional tactical techniques and unwavering courage that would define this critical moment in his military service.

The German party of 25 armed men swiftly approached the American forces, catching them off guard. Noticing this attack, Johnson immediately responded, exhibiting his exceptional situational awareness skills and split-second decision-making. The odds were against the defenders, with the enemy holding numerical and tactical superiority. Yet, Johnson chose not to retreat but to resist, setting the stage for a display of extraordinary heroism.

With a rifle and a bolo knife, Johnson engaged the enemy in close-quarters combat with a ferocity that showed true grit and defied the chaos around him. When the ammunition ran out, he used his knife and the empty rifle as a club to inflict damage. Military veterans quote Johnson's use of the bolo knife as an example of improvising during combat and using non-conventional weapons to deliver the most impact. This unconventional approach disrupted the German raiding party's cohesion, buying crucial time for his fellow soldiers and turning the tide of the skirmish.

As the intensity of the conflict escalated, Johnson's resourcefulness again came to the fore. In a desperate move, he threw hand grenades with precision to repel the enemy and break the attack's intensity. The strategic use of explosives demonstrated Johnson's ability to leverage available resources under extreme pressure, turning the tide of the battle in the Americans' favor.

Johnson's commitment to his fellow soldier, Needham Roberts, throughout the harrowing engagement was unwavering. Despite sustaining multiple injuries, Johnson fought courageously to shield Roberts from harm, showing the real spirit of brotherhood shared within the Harlem Hellfighters. This unwavering commitment to ensure his comrades' well-being amid the chaos of battle is a rare gift.

The price of Johnson's heroic defense was significant, as he endured gunshot wounds, cuts, scrapes, and other injuries from the enemy's weapons. However, his resilience remained undiminished, and the sacrifices made during this nighttime raid became a defining chapter in Johnson's legacy. His strategic brilliance, resourcefulness, and unwavering commitment to duty illuminated the darkness of the trenches, forging a narrative of courage and resilience of the Harlem

Hellfighters.

The Aftermath

The aftermath of Henry Johnson's heroic stand unfolded as a testament to the physical and symbolic costs of his unwavering courage in the face of overwhelming odds. Having repelled the German raiding party in the trenches of the Western Front, Johnson emerged from the event as a wounded but resolute figure. His injuries, which consisted of several gunshot wounds and numerous strikes from the enemy's weapons, bore witness to the ferocity of the hand-to-hand combat he had bravely undertaken. The toll on his body became a tangible representation of the sacrifices made during the battle, underscoring the conflict's brutal nature in which he had engaged.

Although he had sustained a substantial amount of injuries, the way he responded to the attack didn't go unnoticed by the allies and enemies. The French allies, renowned for their appreciation of acts of bravery, swiftly recognized the extraordinary heroism displayed by the Harlem Hellfighter. In a gesture of appreciation for his acts, the French government awarded Johnson the Croix de Guerre, a prestigious military decoration reserved for those who exhibited exceptional bravery in the face of the enemy. This recognition from a nation with a deep historical connection to the ideals of liberty and equality elevated Johnson's heroism to an international stage.

The French commendation boosted Johnson's acts of war on multiple levels. It formally acknowledged Johnson's bravery, recognizing his exceptional contributions on the battlefield. Furthermore, it highlighted the stark contrast between the recognition bestowed by the French and the racial prejudices prevalent in the United States. The wounds he endured during the harrowing night raid became a symbol of resilience and defiance. These wounds depicted the story of a soldier who stood firm against all odds in defense of his comrades and the Nation. The French Croix de Guerre proudly displayed on Johnson's uniform represented more than a military decoration. It became a beacon of hope, challenging the prevailing racial injustices and advocating for a recognition of heroism irrespective of skin color.

In World War I history, the immediate aftermath of Henry Johnson's heroic stand became a narrative of sacrifice, recognition, and a powerful challenge to the societal norms of the time. His injuries and the French commendation created a poignant chapter in the broader struggle for equality, justice, and acknowledgment of the remarkable contributions of black soldiers in a war that reshaped the contours of the world.

Recognition after War

Although Johnson had received a commendation from the French government, recognition of Johnson's wartime achievements was not the same at home. There were stark disparities in treatment based on race during the early 20th century in the United States. Johnson's experience reflects the complex interplay between international acclaim and domestic neglect, highlighting the broader issues of racial discrimination and inequality people of color faced in predominantly white countries.

In France, Johnson was acknowledged for his heroism on equal footing with his white counterparts. The irony was that a nation across the Atlantic, sharing values of liberty and equality with the United States, was more swift and willing to honor Johnson than his homeland.

Upon returning to the United States, Johnson encountered a different reality. The racial climate, marked by deeply ingrained discrimination and segregation, denied him the recognition he rightfully deserved. The stark difference between the hero's welcome he received in France and the lack of acknowledgment at home highlighted the disturbing reality that racial biases persisted within American society, even among those who had fought side by side in the war.

The struggle for recognition at home became a protracted ordeal, mirroring the broader challenges faced by African American soldiers. Johnson's heroism did not shield him from the racial injustices prevalent within the very nation he had served. The delay in acknowledging his contributions underscored the systemic barriers that hindered the same treatment of black soldiers, perpetuating a narrative of inequality and marginalization.

His discharge records didn't mention the injuries he sustained during the war, and he failed to receive recognition and was even denied a disability allowance. Soon, he resumed his job as a porter but couldn't continue due to his injuries and educational constraints. Johnson died at the age of 32 of myocarditis.

It wasn't until 1996 that President Bill Clinton awarded Johnson a military award, the Purple Heart, for his war efforts. Following this medal, the second-highest award, the Distinguished Service Cross, was awarded in 2003. This award in 2003 was received by Herman A. Johnson, who at the time was believed to be his family member. In 2015, nearly a century after his heroic stand, Henry Johnson posthumously received the Medal of Honor from the U.S. government, a belated recognition that sought to rectify historical oversights. The 44th President of the United States, Barack Obama, presented this prestigious award to Sergeant Major Louis Wilson. This long-delayed acknowledgment reflected a broader societal reckoning with the historical treatment of black soldiers and the imperative to correct the record.

The courage of African American soldiers on the battlefield did not shield them from the racial prejudices prevalent within their country. Although Johnson received the long-awaited praise, the delayed recognition is a reminder of the ongoing work required to address historical injustices and ensure the contributions of all soldiers, regardless of race, are duly celebrated and honored.

In the annals of military history, the battle that unfolded on May 14-15, 1918, in the trenches of the Western Front is a testament to the indomitable spirit and extraordinary courage of Henry Johnson, the Harlem Hellfighter. Johnson's heroic stand against overwhelming odds, marked by tactical brilliance, resourcefulness, and unwavering courage, became a defining moment in his journey and of racial dynamics and recognition during World War I. The scars on his body, a legacy of the intense hand-to-hand combat, bore witness to the sacrifices made in the crucible of war.

The French commendation, a swift acknowledgment of his heroism, starkly contrasted with the prolonged struggle for recognition at home. Henry Johnson's battle accompanied the complexities of race, sacrifice, and the enduring quest for justice, leaving an indelible mark on the narrative of African American soldiers whose once-overlooked contributions now demand acknowledgment and appreciation. His legacy is a reminder that the actual cost of war extends beyond the battlefield, often entwined with the persistent struggle for equality and recognition.

Chapter 8: Fay Howe: The Lighthouse Keeper's Daughter

Throughout history, you will read about stories that will make you pause and reflect on how generous and kind one person can be. This is one of these stories. Fay Howe was a young girl with innocent and tender facial expressions that reflected her true and kind nature.

Although Fay's story was touching as she made a difference in thousands of Australian soldiers' lives, not many people knew about her. She was only known to the men whom she helped during the war. Luckily, her only son shed light on her life and offered information on this incredible woman.

This chapter takes you on an adventure to Breaksea Island, Australia, to discover Fay Howe's tireless work aiding AIF (Australian Imperial Force) ships waiting near the lighthouse where the young girl, whose mother had died, lived with her father.

Fay Howe Upbringing

Born in 1899 at Cape Leeuwin Lighthouse, Fay was the daughter of Robert and Hannah Howe. She was the youngest of four siblings: Harold, Evelyn, and Ada. When Fay turned six, her father moved to Breaksea Island with his wife and Fay, leaving his other children in Albany to attend school. Robert was a lighthouse keeper, earning Fay's famous name "The Light Keeper's Daughter." She had an interesting upbringing, and her father taught her unique skills that many girls her age didn't have.

Fay Howe was born at Cape Leeuwin Lighthouse.

From a young age, she could use a gun and hunt rabbits and birds to provide for her family. Her parents taught her to read, write, sew, crochet, cook, do arithmetic, telegraphy and Morse code, semaphore, and signal with flags. Fay learned these skills, became proficient at them, and grew up confident and extremely capable. Her parents were extremely proud of her. Fay had a warm and loving upbringing, but it wasn't without its hardships and sad moments.

Life on the island was tough. During bad weather, Fay and her family struggled to make ends meet because supply boats only came once a month.

At 13, she became an aunt when her sister Ada gave birth to her first child, a boy named Stanley. Sadly, their joy didn't last long, as Ada died soon after the birth. Stanley was sent to Breaksea Island so his grandmother, Hannah, could care for him. However, she died less than a year later, and Fay, who was a child herself, was left to raise him.

Fay's life turned upside down. Not only was she taking care of a baby, but she was also helping her father run the lighthouse while mourning the loss of her beloved mother. Fortunately, she was prepared for the role. She used everything her parents had taught her to create a home for her father and nephew. However, something was about to happen that would change her life forever.

The First World War started in 1914, right after Hannah's death. The events taking place during this period cemented Fay's name in history.

Fay Howe's Heroism

In 1914, about 30,000 Australian soldiers arrived on the island. They were young men, some in their twenties, while others were only teenagers. Each was holding a wildflower given to them by the people of Australia and New Zealand to wish them a safe trip before sailing to Europe and Egypt.

The soldiers waited off the coast for a few days before setting sail. The ships stood a few miles away from where Fay lived. However, some historians believe the ships were closer than initially thought, as the sailors appeared to be able to see her as she waved her flags or sent signals.

The uncertainty of the war impacted the soldiers differently. Some were excited for their adventure, while others were afraid, not knowing what to expect. The lighthouse keeper's daughter, Fay, watched from a distance as they made their way to and from the island and was in awe of the men risking their lives for their country. She could sense the fear in the young boy's hearts, yet she was impressed by their bravery. She had always wondered if there was anything she could do to help them.

The soldiers were prohibited from leaving the ships. However, they desperately wanted to get in touch with their families to let them know they were alive. Some sent messages in bottles, hoping they would reach their loved ones. Other soldiers decided on another method.

They could see Fay watching them and hoped she would help them. Since she knew Morse code and semaphore, she became their messenger. They signaled her when they needed to send messages, and she would deliver them immediately.

From a small island far away from the big city, Fay used undersea cable and telegraph to send the soldiers messages to their loved ones. She would bring their families' replies to the eager men using semaphore flags and Morse code. One can only imagine how the soldiers felt during that time. They were desperate to send their last words to their families and trusted Fay to deliver these messages. They were their most vulnerable selves with her and weren't afraid to show their weaknesses. Fay didn't disappoint – and became the only link these soldiers had to their families back home.

However, some didn't have any family or friends, but they found companionship with Fay. Fay needed these men as much as they needed her. There weren't many people on the island, and her father worked all day. She only had her pigs, a dog, and two donkeys for company. She felt lonely and longed for human companionship, so she was excited to communicate with the soldiers and their families. However, this wasn't the only reason Faye helped the soldiers. She was driven by a sense of duty and love for her country. World War I was the first time Australia had gone to war, and it was a significant time in its history.

Interestingly, the soldiers never met Fay in person, but they were grateful for everything she did for them. It is believed that they bonded with her. Since they were stuck on the ship all day, it would make sense that they spent their time signaling her.

Many expressed their gratitude by sending Fay postcards from the battlegrounds. They never knew her name, so they addressed their letters to "The Little Girl on Breaksea Island."

Fay was so moved by this lovely gesture that she kept all the postcards. When her youngest son Don was a child, he went through them, not knowing their significance or what they meant. When he was interviewed a few years ago, he said there were "dozens and dozens" of postcards. They had tales of the soldiers' lives and their experiences on the battlefield. He believed his mother had written back to them, but he didn't know how many letters she had sent. Sadly, many of the soldiers' postcards were lost.

When the soldiers were ready to head to battle, Fay would wave and wish them good luck, hoping they would return home safely. She became the last person to communicate with the soldiers and the last face they saw before they left for war. She symbolized what these young men were fighting for and protecting.

They never forgot the young girl they saw on Breaksea Island and her kindness. Her memory was engraved in their hearts, a constant reminder of the goodness of the people waiting for them to return victorious.

Although Fay was raising her baby nephew, cooking for the lighthouse keepers, and washing their clothes, she didn't hesitate to give her time and energy to the soldiers and provide consolation. She knew many wouldn't return home, and she was happy to bring them comfort and put a smile on their faces one last time.

Fay's Life after the War

Fay didn't have a simple life. She experienced more pain and heartbreak after her mother's and sister's deaths. A year after the soldiers left, Fay fell in love with a man, James, who was 19 years older than her, and she became pregnant with their first child. James was also a lighthouse keeper and worked with her father. Fay and James got married and moved to Perth. They first lived with James' parents for a few years before saving money and moving to East Fremantle, where Fay spent the rest of her life.

Sadly, she lost her first two sons, one just a couple of hours after he was born and the other when he was a little over a year old. She later had two daughters, Doreen and Marjory, and a son, Don.

James died in 1946, leaving Fay as the breadwinner of the family. She became a wardress at Fremantle Prison but wasn't making enough money to support her family, so she worked as a dressmaker for extra income. Fay became a father and mother for her children. She raised three beautiful and successful children thanks to her strong will and can-do attitude that was apparent during the war.

In 1968, Fay passed away at the age of 68 after suffering a stroke, leaving behind her three children and nine grandchildren.

Don Watson

You can't talk about Fay Howe without mentioning her son, Don, who narrated his mother's story and provided the information mentioned in this chapter. Don knew his mother was a war heroine even though he knew little about her history. He said she preferred to keep that part of her life to herself and rarely talked about her special bond with the soldiers.

He remembered watching his mother going through the old postcards with a smile on her face and tears in her eyes, thinking of all the soldiers who never came back home. He was always touched by her story and how she could still remember and miss these soldiers after all those years.

He imagined her sending messages to their worried families and friends, letting them know the soldiers were fine and alive. Deep down, he knew his kind-hearted mother found joy in telling the soldiers that their families missed them and couldn't wait for them to come home.

Don was proud of his mother and her role during that dark time. She was a child then, yet she managed to ease the worries of thousands of soldiers and their families.

He visited Breaksea Island some years later for the first time in his life, and he couldn't help but feel a connection to the place where his mother had made history. He was overcome with emotion, standing where his mother had stood decades ago.

Fay's story has become popular in the last few years and has become a book and a play.

Not every hero must fight and bleed. Some are just good people who make a difference in the world with kindness. Fay became a heroine for her good heart and willingness to help others without expecting anything in return. She was a beacon of hope for these men, offering them one last chance to communicate with their families, say their last goodbyes, and say, "I love you."

Chapter 9: Nurse Helen Fairchild: Belle of the Battlefield

Amid the harrowing landscapes of the Western Front during World War I, this chapter highlights the profound story of the famed nurse Helen Fairchild, whose selfless service impacted the annals of wartime healthcare. Operating in conditions marked by chaos, scarcity, and the unrelenting toll of conflict, Fairchild's relentless dedication to her patients became a beacon of compassion in the darkness of war.

Nurse Helen Fairchild's service impacted the annals of wartime healthcare.
National Library of Scotland, No restrictions, via Wikimedia Commons:
https://commons.wikimedia.org/wiki/File:WAAC%27s_in_France_find_German_helmets_useful_substitutes_for_market_bags_(3016320811).jpg

Nurse Fairchild fearlessly navigated the grim realities of the Western Front, where the echoes of artillery engulfed makeshift hospitals and the overpowering scent of antiseptics mingled with the pungent odor of sweat, tears, and blood from battle. Under the constant threat of enemy attacks, Fairchild worked tirelessly to provide comfort and care to the wounded and dying. The makeshift medical facilities, overcrowded by the sheer volume of casualties, became a significant motivator to her unwavering commitment as she excelled under challenging circumstances with an unshaken spirit.

While her relentless efforts to provide medical care to the wounded and vulnerable were praised during World War I, her courage, determination, and priority to provide emergency medical care were only recognized when she was appointed to a front-line station during the Battle of Ypres. This was when the third battle of Ypres began, and nurses were required at the front line to provide adequate care to the wounded and deal with medical emergencies. Surgical teams were prepared and sent to the casualty clearing stations to give emergency medical care. Each team had a surgeon, an anesthetist, a nurse, and a sergeant. Surgical teams stayed in the causality clearing station for not more than 48 hours. However, this time was different, as Helen Fairchild and her team stayed for five weeks before receiving medical supplies or having access to clean clothing.

Her relentless dedication extended beyond the call of duty, as she not only tended to physical wounds but also comforted soldiers grappling with the trauma of war. Fairchild's soothing words and compassionate gestures were a balm to the psychological scars. She stood as a pillar of strength, offering a glimmer of humanity amid the brutality of conflict.

The shortage of medical supplies and the relentless demand for care meant that she typically worked with limited resources. The strain on her well-being compounded her tireless efforts as exhaustion became a constant companion in her quest to provide comfort in suffering. The stories of soldiers whose lives she touched attested to the transformative power of her care, illustrating the essence of selflessness during the war.

Tragically, Fairchild's tale took a poignant turn as her untimely demise marked the ultimate sacrifice made in service to others. The toll of war, visible and unseen, claimed this dedicated nurse, underscoring the profound costs borne by those who tended to the wounded in the theater of conflict. Fairchild's legacy became a symbol of the resilience and compassion of wartime caregivers, a narrative of courage and sacrifice etched into history.

In this chapter, the story of Nurse Fairchild on the Western Front is no less than a testament to the immeasurable impact of selfless service in adversity. Her dedication, sacrifices, and untimely demise are a sad reminder of the human cost of war and the enduring legacy of those who, in the darkest hours, exemplify the true meaning of compassion and heroism.

Helen's Impact on Medical Care

Nurse Fairchild's impact on medical care during World War I was nothing short of transformational, as her unwavering dedication and exceptional skills inspired the front-line healthcare system to improvise and make changes for better care in the coming years. Operating in the challenging and chaotic environment of the Western Front, Fairchild became a beacon of compassion, resilience, and innovation, elevating the standard of care for the wounded and setting a precedent for wartime medical service.

Nurse Fairchild showed remarkable resourcefulness in conditions where the scarcity of medical supplies, food, water, and related amenities was evident. Due to a medical supply shortage, she improvised, adapting to the circumstances with ingenuity and efficiency. Her ability to make do with limited resources sustained the operations of the medical facilities and ensured the wounded received the care they desperately needed. Fairchild's resourcefulness became symbolic of the adaptability required during wartime challenges.

Despite the shortage of medical supplies, Fairchild recognized the profound psychological toll that war exacted on soldiers and incorporated elements of emotional support into her caregiving. In a landscape where mental health was often overlooked, she provided solace and comfort, creating an environment of healing for the psychological scars of war. Fairchild's holistic approach to medical care demonstrated a keen understanding of the interconnectedness of physical and mental well-being, especially for soldiers on active duty.

Furthermore, Fairchild's tireless dedication set a high standard for her colleagues. Her relentless work ethic and commitment to her patients inspired those around her, creating a culture of excellence within the medical teams. The ripple effect of her influence contributed to an elevated level of professionalism and compassion among wartime medical practitioners, shaping the ethos of caregiving on the front lines.

Although the letters she wrote to her family were upbeat, the conditions she worked in were unimaginable. Here is an example that describes the conditions: As the medical camps and tents were on the front line, one of the tents got hit by a bomb, injuring a staff nurse's eye. The operation was performed while standing on a muddy terrain with only a flashlight as the light source.

Tragically, Nurse Fairchild's untimely demise marked the ultimate sacrifice made in the pursuit of advancing medical care during wartime. However, her impact endured beyond her physical presence, serving as a testament to the enduring legacy of those who, through their selfless service, redefine the boundaries of medical care in the most challenging circumstances.

In the history books of wartime healthcare, Nurse Fairchild's impact is a testament to the resilience, innovation, and compassion that can flourish even in the harshest conditions. Her contributions became a guiding light for subsequent generations of healthcare professionals, embodying the spirit of those who, in the crucible of war, redefine medical care possibilities and leave an enduring legacy of compassion and excellence.

Passion Fueling Goals

Nurse Fairchild's journey into the nursing profession was intricately interwoven with early inspirations to serve humanity and an innate drive to alleviate suffering, creating a compassionate nature and bestowing her with a deep sense of purpose. Fairchild was born into a family with a strong tradition of service and empathy, so her childhood was shaped by the values of compassion and commitment to helping others.

Growing up in a community that prioritized collective well-being, Fairchild witnessed firsthand the impact of individuals who dedicated their lives to the service of others. Whether it was family members tending to ailing neighbors or community leaders organizing support for those in need, these early exposures instilled in Fairchild a profound understanding of the transformative power of compassion and care.

Fairchild's interactions with healthcare professionals fueled her aspirations as she navigated her formative years. Inspired by the nurses and doctors who tirelessly worked to alleviate suffering, she developed a keen interest in medicine. Her visits to local clinics and hospitals, often accompanying family members seeking medical care, became significant experiences igniting her passion for healing and a desire to contribute to the well-being of others.

Upon reaching adulthood, Fairchild's decision to pursue nursing was a natural extension of her lifelong commitment to making treatment accessible and alleviating suffering. Driven by a profound sense of empathy and a desire to improve the lives of those with health challenges, she embarked on a rigorous nursing education journey with unwavering determination.

Her journey into the nursing profession was not merely a career choice but a calling reflective of her deeply ingrained beliefs. This determination and motivation she harnessed from her aspirations would define Nurse Fairchild's exceptional contributions on the Western Front during World War I, where her compassionate spirit and commitment to alleviating suffering became a beacon of hope during the chaotic war.

In the trenches spread throughout the Western Front during World War I, Nurse Fairchild forged an unbreakable bond of trust with her fellow nurses, creating a collective spirit and determination of resilience despite the relentless challenges of war. The bond among these healthcare professionals transcended the traditional notions of companionship, evolving into a sisterhood bound by a shared purpose: to bring comfort and healing to those engulfed by the conflict.

Together, they navigated the makeshift hospitals, worked tirelessly through the long and arduous hours, and faced the emotional toll of witnessing the suffering of countless soldiers. This shared experience gave the nurses an unspoken understanding of each other, a silent acknowledgment of their collective burdens. In the scarcity and adversity, they leaned on each other, creating an environment where each nurse's strengths compensated for the weaknesses of the other. The synergy among these healthcare professionals exemplified the power of teamwork in the most challenging circumstances.

This environment became essential in sustaining their morale and fortitude despite the constant inflow of wounded soldiers seeking care. In the dimly lit and emotionally charged environment of the medical facilities, Fairchild and her colleagues became coworkers and pillars of support for one another. Together, they embodied the collective determination defining their noble mission amid the chaos and suffering of World War I.

Innovative Makeshift Techniques

In the challenging environment of the Western Front during World War I, Nurse Fairchild's ingenuity and resourcefulness shone through as she navigated the scarcity of medical supplies. Faced with insufficient resources, Fairchild became a pioneer in improvisation, employing innovative and makeshift techniques to provide essential care to the wounded soldiers under her charge.

One of Fairchild's notable innovations was her adept use of locally available materials as substitutes for conventional medical supplies. Lacking access to an abundance of bandages and sterile dressings, she ingeniously repurposed items like clean, torn linens and pieces of cloth to create makeshift bandages. This resourceful approach conserved precious supplies and ensured the wounded received the necessary wound care despite the limitations. Tin cans, sterilized under makeshift conditions, became impromptu containers for sterilizing and storing medical instruments. Fairchild's ability to transform ordinary items into essential medical tools underscored her adaptability and determination to overcome the constraints imposed by wartime shortages.

Fairchild's innovations didn't stop at makeshift bandages and improvised instruments. She also pioneered creative wound care techniques. Recognizing the necessity of maintaining cleanliness in the crowded and unsanitary conditions of the trenches, she devised alternative methods for wound irrigation, often relying on distilled water procured through inventive means. These improvised hygiene practices were crucial in preventing infections and promoting healing.

Her resourcefulness was also evident in her strategic use of available space within the makeshift hospitals. Crates, barrels, and other repurposed containers were transformed into makeshift medical storage units, allowing her to organize and locate essential supplies efficiently. The efficient use of space became a hallmark of her ability to create functional medical environments despite the challenging circumstances.

In the absence of specialized medical equipment, Fairchild's diagnostic skills and hands-on approach became critical skills. She relied on her clinical judgment and expertise to assess and address medical issues, emphasizing a personalized and attentive approach to each patient. This human-centric method compensated for the lack of technological advancements and underscored the compassionate nature of her caregiving.

Nurse Fairchild's ability to innovate in adversity symbolized resilience on the Western Front. Her makeshift techniques and resourceful strategies addressed immediate medical needs and set a precedent for creative problem-solving in healthcare. Fairchild's ingenuity sustained medical operations in the trenches but became a prime example of the unwavering commitment of healthcare professionals to adapt and overcome, even in the most challenging circumstances.

Personal Accounts of War

Amid the disarray and suffering of the Western Front, the impact of Nurse Fairchild's empathetic approach and unwavering dedication resonated deeply with the soldiers who received treatment and care from her. Personal accounts from these soldiers paint a vivid picture of the compassionate and tireless nurse who became a beacon of comfort amid the horrors of war.

Private James Anderson, a soldier wounded during a skirmish, reported his experience under Nurse Fairchild's care with utmost gratitude. He spoke of her calming presence, describing how her soothing words and gentle touch comforted and encouraged him during excruciating pain. Despite being on the front line, these healthcare professionals aimed to provide exceptional care. Anderson noted that Fairchild's empathetic approach went beyond physical care. She took the time to listen to the soldiers' fears and concerns, offering medical attention and a compassionate ear in a desolate environment.

Sergeant Thomas Mitchell incurred a severe leg injury during a skirmish. He vividly remembered the time Nurse Fairchild treated him with exceptional dedication. Despite the overwhelming workload and limited resources, Mitchell recounted how Fairchild tirelessly tended his wound, rinsed it with distilled water, and applied adequate bandages to stop the bleeding. Her commitment to providing personalized care stood out, leaving a lasting impression on Mitchell and reinforcing the soldiers' belief that they were more than just casualties. They were individuals deserving of compassion and respect.

Another army man named Private Robert Johnson, injured from a gunshot wound, spoke of the impact of Fairchild's emotional support. He recounted how Fairchild's empathetic words and genuine concern gave him a lifeline in moments of despair and homesickness. Johnson emphasized that Fairchild's role extended beyond the medical. She became a source of emotional resilience, giving hope in the despair that pervaded the medical facilities.

Besides these reported accounts, countless soldiers were treated and provided adequate care while Helen stayed on duty. Her team also reported her efforts. Corporal Sarah Turner, a nurse colleague of Fairchild, attested to her remarkable leadership and mentorship. Turner described Fairchild as a guiding force, always ready to share her innovative techniques and medical insights with the nursing team. Turner highlighted Fairchild's ability to uplift the spirits of patients and fellow healthcare professionals, creating an environment that served as a beacon of hope in the grim realities of war.

Her dedication exceeded the call of duty, leaving an enduring impact on the soldiers fortunate enough to experience her compassionate approach to healing on the tumultuous Western Front.

Challenges of War-Induced Medical Conditions

Nurse Fairchild's adaptability and resilience were put to the test as the Western Front introduced new and devastating challenges in the war-induced medical conditions, notably gas poisoning and shell shock. In these evolving traumas, she demonstrated a remarkable ability to adapt her caregiving approach to address the complex and often invisible wounds inflicted by modern warfare.

Gas poisoning, a sinister consequence of chemical warfare, presented unprecedented challenges for medical professionals. As these methods of chemical warfare were new in WWI, there was a lack of specialized antidotes or established treatment protocols to address the challenges and complications that gas poisoning could induce. These novel acts of war demanded innovative responses. Drawing on her resourcefulness, Fairchild implemented improvised methods to alleviate the symptoms of gas exposure. Her quick thinking and adaptability in the absence of specific remedies became instrumental in relieving afflicted soldiers, showing her commitment to staying ahead of the ever-changing landscape of war-induced medical conditions.

Although the deaths caused by chemical warfare were less than one percent, the fear of suffering from these gases was instilled in the soldiers. In these desperate times, hearing comforting words gave the soldiers courage and reduced their psychological trauma. Exposure to mustard gas resulted in blisters and skin burns upon contact. The gas fumes, when inhaled, cause lung damage. The toxins from the gas also caused evident liver damage. Thousands of men passed through the causality stations daily, drenched in mustard gas. The liquid-contaminated clothes affected the nurses, exposing them to mustard gas as they were responsible for removing clothes and tending to injuries. Later, an autopsy revealed that the liver damage Fairchild endured was partly due to mustard gas exposure.

Shell shock, a term used during World War I to describe the psychological toll of combat, emerged as another formidable challenge. The mental and emotional wounds inflicted by the constant shelling and exposure to the horrors of war required a nuanced and compassionate approach. Fairchild recognized the need to adapt her caregiving techniques to address the invisible psychological scars left by shell shock. She became an advocate for mental health support, incorporating therapeutic interventions and emotional counseling into her caregiving methods.

Furthermore, as the prevalence of these war-induced medical conditions increased, Fairchild took a proactive role in educating her nursing team about the evolving nature of the traumas experienced by soldiers. Her leadership tailored an environment of continuous learning and adaptation, ensuring the nursing staff remained equipped to provide comprehensive care to those facing the multifaceted challenges of modern warfare.

The adaptability displayed by Nurse Fairchild when dealing with mustard gas poisoning and shell shock exemplified her dedication to staying abreast of the dynamic nature of war traumas. Her willingness to embrace innovative approaches and advocacy for holistic care reinforced the notion that the medical profession must evolve alongside the changing conflict landscape. Fairchild's adaptability became a source of hope and healing in the crucible of war, demonstrating that under her watchful care, even in the most challenging circumstances, compassionate care could be tailored to address the diverse and evolving needs of the soldiers.

Although Fairchild had a relentless passion for providing care and medical treatment to the wounded on the front line, she had medical issues that went unnoticed. Fairchild had a history of abdominal pain, which gradually increased during her time on the front line. Right before Christmas of 1917, she experienced severe abdominal pain and several other symptoms, including vomiting and diarrhea. On further evaluation and an x-ray examination, a gastric ulcer was spotted at the lower opening of the stomach.

In January 1918, Fairchild underwent surgery and was making an excellent recovery but suddenly lapsed into a coma and died. A further post-mortem examination revealed that her liver had developed complications from the inhaled chloroform used for anesthesia during emergency surgical procedures and the mustard gas used during the battle. Nonetheless, courageous and determined individuals like Helen Fairchild gave everything to protect their homeland and turn the tides in their favor.

Chapter 10: Lance Corporal Albert Jacka: Australia's First Victoria Cross

This final chapter in the World War I biographies chronicles the acts of valor that made Lance Corporal Albert Jacka Australia's first recipient of the Victoria Cross during World War I. Detailing the specific actions, decisions, and battles that demonstrated his exceptional bravery and leadership on the front line, this chapter explores Jacka's formative years in Victoria, Australia, drawing connections between his rugged upbringing and his battlefield prowess and highlighting his leadership instincts, which he honed even before his recognition, an act that endeared him to fellow soldiers. You'll read about the Gallipoli campaign and the intricate details of trench warfare that marked Jacka's heroics and led to his Victoria Cross award despite the overwhelming odds he faced.

Albert Jacka was Australia's first recipient of the Victoria Cross during World War I.

https://commons.wikimedia.org/wiki/File:Albert_Jacka_portrait_P02939.001.jpg

Albert Jacka's Formative Years

Born in January 1893 in Victoria, Australia, Albert Jacka was the son of Nathaniel Jacka, a dairy farmer and a contractor with Victoria's mines and railways. Besides engaging in different athletic pursuits, like cycling and boxing, young Albert also worked for his father after finishing elementary school. Later, he applied for service in the Victorian State Forests Department, where he was employed until World War I. After the cataclysmic events that sparked and then spread the war, the Australian Imperial Force was established. Albert Jacka enlisted soon after, and by mid-September 1914, he was training with the 14th Battalion. A month later, his unit was sent to England to complete their training before being deployed to the Western Front. However, plans changed due to the unexpected Turkish alliance with the Germans, and Jacka's division was sent to Egypt. Initially, they were only sent for further training and as reserve assistance for the Suez Canal defense.

Developing Leadership Instincts

During their preparation period, the Australian unit was training alongside other divisions, which had stricter approaches to discipline. Due to this, Jacka's unit was initially seen as very undisciplined and defiant to authority. However, this soon changed as Jacka took the initiative to implement a more aggressive leadership style, which inspired loyalty. He showed and encouraged valor during training, which made his men respect him even more. Even his enemies spoke of him with fear. He was described as outspoken and lacking tolerance for rowdiness, and at the same time, he didn't have much diplomacy or finesse. While this didn't earn him any favors from his superiors, it cemented his reputation among his men, which ultimately mattered on the battlefield. By the time his unit joined the New Zealand brigades and formed the New Zealand and Australian Division led by General Alexander Godley, Jacka's Mob (as they were known) was a well-organized unit ready to fight. This was good because they would soon get their first taste of war and embark on one of history's most controversial military campaigns.

The Gallipoli Campaign

From April 26, 1915, Albert Jacka's battalion was stationed at Gallipoli, where it continued training. The Turkish soon closed in on the area where the New Zealand and Australian Division were and launched an attack, trying to drive them back toward the sea. The Australian soldiers were pushed back to the narrow shoreline as they engaged in battle with the enemy. Despite having less than an hour to prepare for the incoming attack, the division defended Courtney's Post (a small sector of their trenches), but the Turkish soldiers occupied its edge. Valiant as ever, Jacka proposed that they attempt to get the entire post back under their control. However, his first attempt to execute a counterattack with full force failed. They had little room to maneuver, and the Turkish had the advantage of knowing the terrain better. The Turkish soldiers easily pinned them down with heavy fire, severely injuring one of the Australian soldiers and wounding several others. Jacka immediately returned to his line.

Realizing that a group couldn't get through, but one person would have a better chance of moving without drawing attention, Jacka charged across the space to reach the Turkish positions. Meanwhile, his commander created a diversion by throwing two grenades and opening fire on the Turks to allow Jacka to go around and surprise the enemy from the rear. Once he reached the trench behind the enemy lines, he started firing and was determined to keep at it until backup arrived. Immediately, he took down two Turkish soldiers with a bayonet and another five with his rifle. Taken by surprise, the rest of the Turks must have thought they were being attacked from their flank by an entire group, so they ran back to their lines, and Jacka was able to hold the trench. His commander arrived a few hours later, finding Jacka calmly waiting for him. For this most conspicuous act of bravery on the night of May 19 and 20, 1915, on the Gallipoli Peninsula, Albert Jacka received the prestigious Victoria Cross Award. It was the first-ever Victory Cross awarded to a member of the Australian Imperial Force in World War I.

However, Jacka and his comrades would engage in many more battles at Gallipoli. In August 1915, they made further attempts to expand their territory from that narrow beach they had occupied in May. Fighting on the rugged terrain at Chunuk Bair, the battalion had another mission to support the British troops arriving at Suvla Bay. These attempts were as successful as the ones before, and nearly 600 men died in the first few days of engaging the Turks. Jacka recorded his frustration in his diary after seeing almost his entire battalion being wiped out. With only 200 men remaining, they were indeed decimated, and this was only the beginning of a period of heavy fighting. Still, even as casualties kept mounting, Jacka thrived on the battlefield. He engaged in several more fights with the Turks, often alone and with little to no backup. Due to his bravery, by the end of August, he was promoted to corporal.

Leaving and Returning to Egypt

After months of arduous struggle, the Australian division and the rest of the Allied soldiers withdrew from Gallipoli in December 1915. By this time, the number of Australian casualties mounted to over 25,000. The Jacka battalion was sent to the island of Lemnos in the Aegean Sea for the holidays but was ordered to return to Egypt in January 1916. Their returning group was organized into smaller brigades by March. When the reorganization was over, Jacka was appointed as a second lieutenant. He had held the title of company sergeant major since mid-November. Once again stationed in Egypt, Jacka was tasked to train officers until he became a second lieutenant in April. In testimonials, comrades and superiors readily expressed their admiration for Jacka's gallantry and unwavering spirit on the front lines of the Great War. Hearing about Jacka's previous feat of single-handedly taking out seven Turkish soldiers, E. J. Rule, a new soldier assigned to his battalion, expected to encounter Jacka, a proud military officer who strove to add more to the prestigious award he received. Instead, he was surprised to find a confident and outspoken soldier with a strong character who had no other aspiration than to fight alongside his comrades. As he began training, the soldier described Jacka as a veritable rock (despite his average, medium build and crooked nose) for his men. Whenever someone started to lose faith or courage amid the fruitless fights, they only needed to look at Jacka's determination to keep going and gain the strength to follow him. The soldier remarked that Jacka's character never changed despite all the promotions and awards he received. His men were thrilled to be part of "Jacka's Mob" because they knew without a doubt that thanks to Jacka, they were part of the strongest 14th Battalion unit of the Australian Imperial Force.

Later Assignments

In mid-1916, Jacka's battalion was deployed to France and entered the war again, this time fighting the Germans. Tasked to draw the German troop's attention away from the British raids on the country's southern side, the Australian battalion engaged in a series of arduous raids. Despite being armed with steel helmets, gas masks, and heavy ammunition, the fighting cost the lives of many Australian soldiers, but the worst was yet to come. Once the Allied forces realized the Somme offensive launched in northern France was about to fail, they sent Jacka's battalion as reinforcement. They arrived at the village of Pozières, which was heavily fortified with German forces and ammunition, including machine gun positions and dugouts. In short, the Germans transformed this formerly sleepy French village into a fortress and successfully defended it against the Allied forces. While the latter did plenty of damage to the German trenches and even forced their front-line units to draw back and find cover in makeshift concealment areas, this came with a heavy cost. Over 50,000 Allied soldiers were lost on the first day of battle.

Executing a masterfully thought-out plan, the Australian Division attacked Pozières and quickly took over the village. While they also suffered over 500 casualties, they fought valiantly and eventually defeated the Germans. Even the most seasoned Australian soldiers described the

Pozières battle as one of the most challenging battles they had fought since entering the war. After the carnage, Jacka was devastated to discover that there were only seven uninjured men left in his command. Moreover, while the Australians had won the battle, they still had to hold onto the village and defend it against the German reinforcement, who arrived with five battalions determined to regain control over Pozières at all costs.

Walking through a dugout with a small group of his soldiers, Jacka realized that the attack had begun when the Germans threw two stick grenades into their unit's territory, wounding two of his soldiers. True to his form, Jacka immediately leaped to the rescue and shot the German guard who had thrown the grenade. Jacka devised a plan involving his men breaking through the German lines and fleeing to meet the rest of their battalion stationed outside the village. However, before they had time to act, Jacka noticed a large group of German soldiers walking toward them, with 40 Australian captives in tow. Jacka calculated the Germans' number to be at least 150. Still, despite this, he once again executed a swift surprise attack that left the enemy confused and quick to surrender, thinking they were being attacked by a group as large as theirs. As the Germans dropped their weapons in surprise, the 40 Australian prisoners picked them up and joined their comrades against the enemy. The other German battalions joined in on the battle, and another vicious fight ensued between the German and the Australian soldiers. When their ammunition ran out, Jacka and his men fought with their fists, taking a heroic stand even after sustaining numerous injuries.

According to the recollection of some of his comrades, Jacka killed between 12 and 20 Germans in hand-to-hand combat. Eventually, the Germans surrendered, but Jacka was thought to have died on the battlefield. Using his force of will, the severely wounded and barely conscious Jacka crawled back to the Australian lines. He was discovered by stretcher-bearers looking for survivors on the battlefield. He was quickly rescued from France and taken to England to recover from his injuries. Albert Jacka received another prestigious award for this highly courageous act, the Military Cross, followed by a bar for his actions at Bullecourt (although some argue that the Pozières feat rivaled Gallipoli and he should have been given a second Victoria Cross instead).

Jacka's actions at Pozières were described daily by Charles Bean, the Official Australian war historian who was present at the French battles. Bean called the quick manner in which Jacka surprised the Germans into surrendering, freed the Australian captives, and fought off the enemy the most effective and dramatic accomplishment in the history of the Australian Imperial Force.

Later, at the events of Bullecourt, Jacka showed great courage once again when he defied his commander, who had ordered an attack on the enemy despite the lack of preparations. Determined to stand up for his men, Jacka advised his commander to work on their plan; otherwise, they would suffer tremendous losses. His warnings were ultimately ignored, and over 2,000 Australian soldiers were killed in the battle. Jacka made several trips into the danger zone, helping Allied soldiers follow through with their advance. He meticulously coached the supporting British tanks into position, further contributing to the Allied victory.

Gaining Fame in His Homeland

Soon after the news of his heroic acts in the first fight at Gallipoli spread in Australia, Jacka quickly rose to fame in his homeland. While he would return home much later, it didn't stop the Australians from featuring him in the news and advertisements, including adverts for military recruiting. Australian businessman John Wren awarded Albert Jacka a gold watch and prize money to accompany his Victoria Cross award. Some local newspapers went as far as describing Jacka as the embodiment of the spirit of the entire New Zealand and Australian Division.

His name was even tied to a conscription-related dilemma. While military training was mandatory for all capable men in Australia, it was only compulsory to serve in domestic territories. Overseas deployment was reserved for volunteers, whose numbers quickly dwindled after World War I broke out. Hearing about the horrors of the European battlefields, few wanted to enter the war. Hence, the Australian government was forced to find new ways to expand its troops. Some initially proposed making overseas service mandatory, but many argued against it. In 1915, Attorney General William Morris Hughes declared that no Australian soldier would be sent to war against their will. However, as recruitment numbers kept declining, he was forced to change his stance, marking the beginning of a nationwide debate. This was when Jacka's fame entered the picture. His name and achievements were boasted across Australia, particularly in Victoria, hoping to use them as an incentive to recruit more soldiers. At the same time, anti-conscriptionists also used his name. Jacka's father belonged to the latter group and campaigned against conscription, which would later cause a divide between him and his son. Jacka's father never agreed to him signing up for the army, so their relationship had been strained since his deployment and deteriorated through the years.

As he rose through the ranks, becoming a captain in the spring of 1917, Jacka received numerous awards and nominations, which only added to his already highly regarded celebrity status. Still, his demeanor remained the same, which, some argue, cost him his climb higher on the military ladder. His outspoken nature wasn't well regarded by his superiors, who expected more finesse from the already seasoned soldier. He didn't care for niceties because his goal was never to chase achievements. He was simply a brave soldier who excelled on the battlefield and became a leader admired by many.

Later Years

After the victory against the Germans, Jacka was asked to return to his homeland and personally partake in recruitment. While the Australian government hoped Jacka would agree to assist the war efforts at home, they were disappointed. Jacka refused the assignment and asked to be sent back to his battalion. He returned to his unit in December 1916 and continued to fight alongside his comrades until mid-1918, when he was gravely wounded and was forced to withdraw from service once and for all. While he sustained multiple injuries in the years prior (including the time he fell unconscious and was thought dead in 1916 and an injury from a sniper's bullet in July 1917), he would recover quickly and continue to serve as an inspiration to young soldiers serving beneath him. However, this injury was debilitating and ultimately put his active military career to an end. Still, even when he couldn't return to battle, his reputation as one of the Australian Imperial Forces' (and possibly the entire New Zealand and Australian Divisions, too) most respected warriors remained.

Jacka returned home for the final time in October 1919. He was received with a grand parade that took him across the streets of Melbourne, with crowds chanting his name and celebrating his achievements. He was officially discharged from military service in early 1920. Jacka and three of his 14th Battalion comrades opened a joint import business. In 1921, Albert Jacka married and continued operating his company until 1930, when the business was liquidated due to the newly imposed highly inflated import taxes meant to counteract the effects of the Depression. Soon after his company was liquidated, Jacka became the mayor of St Kilda. It was a great responsibility, especially in the devastating, poverty-ruled, Depression-era Australia. Yet, he approached it with the same determination as his military assignments. He strove to help those who had lost their employment due to the Depression and used his fame and political connections to assist those who needed help sustaining their families. The mounting number of responsibilities, coupled with the numerous injuries he received through his military service, took a toll on this war hero's health. In mid-December 1931, Jacka was hospitalized, and a month later, he passed away at the age of 39. His burial in St Kilda was conducted with full Military Honors and in the presence of eight Victoria Cross recipients who honored him by acting as pallbearers at his funeral.

Conclusion

Being a hero is a title that cannot be placed on someone without due consideration. The sacrifices and selflessness to defend their countries and ideals make the heroes of WWI unique, especially considering they were navigating the unknown territory of global conflict. They stepped into peak danger, taking dramatic wins and earth-shattering losses. Many gave their lives flying the banners of their units, countries, or squadrons.

Melting into the faceless void of the grand narrative is a fate met by many unsung heroes. The names of some of the brave people who died in the First World War are lost to the passage of time. Accolades, adventures, tribulations, and victories are recorded, but they are not always mentioned in the discussion of the Great War. It would be a tragedy if they were entirely forgotten, so society must keep the war heroes' names alive out of respect for their sacrifices to build the modern world.

WWI ushered in an era of global governance and the development of rules of engagement. The institutions built during and following the war were not 100% effective, considering another world war would occur. However, they were a step in the right direction for building a peaceful and more tolerant world. The project is still ongoing, so highlighting the brightest parts of the human spirit is essential so it can shine onto the broader civilization's psyche and propel people into a world maximizing the well-being of its global citizens. This may seem naive, but there must be an ideological target for humanity to aim at.

The selflessness, resilience, and courage exhibited by the heroes of the Great War cannot be denied. Highlighting the individual stories of these incredible people exposes the human side of war. Reading numbers and cold, hard facts on a screen does not capture the conflict's tragedy. The reality of war is that people get rewarded and praised for killing other people because global governments cannot come to diplomatic solutions. Throughout history, war is an inevitable part of the human experience. However, the inevitability of war does not bury the heartbreaking carnage and widespread loss it causes on so many levels.

The impacts of WWI are still felt today because it marked the shift from the imperial age to the era of nation-states. As civilization strives to build fair systems representing the common people, the everyday folks who dedicated their lives to achieving those ends in brutal conflict must be appreciated. Take this book as a guide to prompt deeper research into the heroic figures who exhibited humanity's highest potential even in the darkest times.

Check out another book in the series

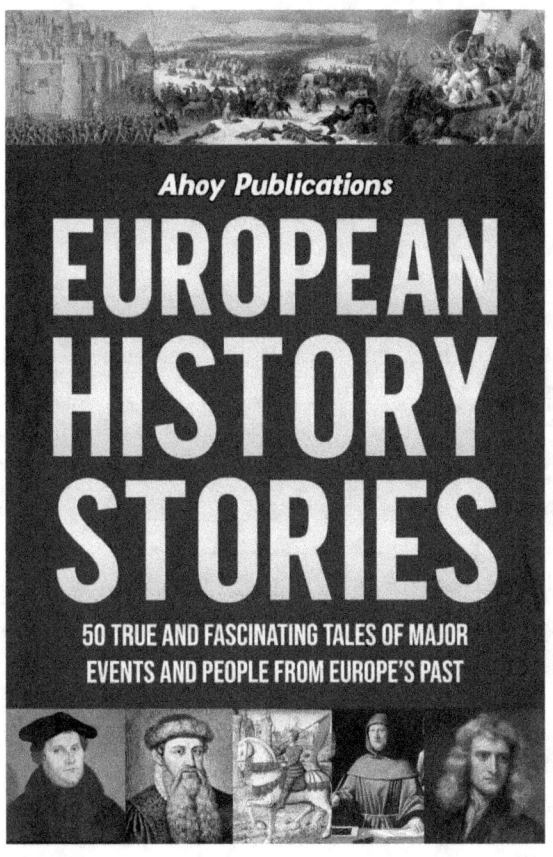

References

(N.d.). Alarabiya.net. https://english.alarabiya.net/perspective/profiles/2013/08/18/The-British-Bedouin-Lawrence-of-Arabia-s-125th-birth-anniversary

(N.d.). Arabnews.com. https://www.arabnews.com/node/305958

(N.d.-a). Fee.org. https://fee.org/articles/the-harlem-hellfighters-the-incredible-story-behind-the-most-decorated-us-regiment-in-world-war-i/

(N.d.-b). Iowa.gov. https://history.iowa.gov/sites/default/files/history-education-nhd-projects-categories-sample-harlem-paper.pdf

"Pat" Pattle. (n.d.). Acesofww2.com. https://acesofww2.com/safrica/aces/pattle/

American Experience. (2017, April 3). The Two Lives of Eugene Bullard. American Experience. https://www.pbs.org/wgbh/americanexperience/features/great-war-two-lives-eugene-bullard/

Andrews, E. (2016, September 16). Ace of aces: How the Red Baron became WWI's most legendary fighter pilot. HISTORY. https://www.history.com/news/ace-of-aces-how-the-red-baron-became-wwis-most-legendary-fighter-pilot

Australia's Venerable Albert Jacka. (2023, September 14). Warfare History Network. https://warfarehistorynetwork.com/article/australias-venerable-albert-jacka/

Bainger, F. (2015, May 25). The lighthouse keeper's daughter. Australian Geographic. https://www.australiangeographic.com.au/topics/history-culture/2015/05/the-lighthouse-keepers-daughter/

Bath, G. (2019, April 25). The story of Fay Howe, the last woman thousands of troops would see before they went to war. Mamamia.

https://www.mamamia.com.au/anzac-day-2019-women/

BEDOUIN CULTURE. (n.d.). Bedawi.com. https://bedawi.com/Bedouin_Culture/

Browne, O. (2006, June 12). T.E. Lawrence: The enigmatic 'Lawrence of Arabia.' HistoryNet. https://www.historynet.com/te-lawrence-the-enigmatic-lawrence-of-arabia/

Butler, S. (2014, July 31). Giant to bring legend to life. Yahoo News. https://au.news.yahoo.com/giant-to-bring-legend-to-life-24602928.html

Byrne, K. (2022, November 11). Meet the American who inspired the nation in two world wars: Christian soldier Sgt. Alvin York. Fox News. https://www.foxnews.com/lifestyle/meet-american-who-inspired-nation-two-world-wars-christian-soldier-sgt-alvin-york

Calitz, G. (2022, January 18). Pat battle - The Commonwealth's Top WWII Ace. Flightlineweekly. https://www.flightlineweekly.com/post/pat-pattle-the-commonwealths-top-wwii-ace

Captain Albert Jacka. (n.d.). Gov.Au. https://www.awm.gov.au/collection/P11033363

Clark, L. (2021, February 24). Tout le Sang Coule Rouge: The Story of Eugene Bullard. Historic America. https://www.historicamerica.org/journal/2021/2/24/tout-le-sang-coule-rouge-the-story-of-eugene-bullard

Cockburn, D. J. (2015, October 21). Inspirations: The legend of Edith Cavell. Cockburn's Eclectics. https://cockburndj.wordpress.com/2015/10/21/inspirations-the-legend-of-edith-cavell/

Dahl, R. (1986). Going Solo. Johnathon Cape.

Demonceau, O. (n.d.). Edith Cavell story - BECCG Brussels Belgium. Edith-Cavell-Belgium.Eu. http://www.edith-cavell-belgium.eu/edith-cavell-story.html

Dickens, P. (n.d.). Marmaduke Pat Pattle –. The Observation Post. https://samilhistory.com/tag/marmaduke-pat-pattle/

Eugene Bullard: boxer, pilot, soldier, spy, and elevator operator. (2017, April 12). Georgia Humanities. https://www.georgiahumanities.org/2017/04/12/eugene-bullard-boxer-fighter-pilot-soldier-spy-and-elevator-operator/

Eugene J. Bullard. (n.d.). Airandspace.si.edu. https://airandspace.si.edu/stories/editorial/eugene-j-bullard

Feloni, R. (2017, August 17). 100 Years Ago, The Real-life Lawrence of Arabia Authored a Leadership Pamphlet Full of Insights That are Still Useful Today. Business Insider. https://www.businessinsider.com/lawrence-of-arabia-leadership-insights-from-27-articles-2017-8

Fraser, H. (2014, January 4). The First World War: Lawrence of Arabia in Jordan. Corinthian Travel Blog. https://www.corinthiantravel.co.uk/blog/the-first-world-war-lawrence-of-arabia-in-jordan/

GM. (2020, September 6). Lawrence of Arabia's Bedouin robes –. Joy of Museums Virtual Tours; JOY of MUSEUMS. https://joyofmuseums.com/museums/united-kingdom-museums/ashmolean/lawrence-of-arabia-bedouin-arab-robes/

Google Arts & Culture. (n.d.). The heroic story of Edith Cavell. Google Arts & Culture. https://artsandculture.google.com/story/the-heroic-story-of-edith-cavell/vwVRDXLK3mGgIQ

Gov, W. A., & Insignia, A. (n.d.). World War I battlefield companion. Abmc.gov. https://www.abmc.gov/sites/default/files/publications/ABMC_WWI%2520Battlefield%2520Companion%2520Book_20180904.pdf

Harvey, I. (2018, August 17). Best allied ace of WWII? - Pat Pattle, South Africa's Most Successful Pilot. Warhistoryonline; War History Online. https://www.warhistoryonline.com/war-articles/south-african-ace-pilot.html

Helen Fairchild. (2016, June 16). Nursing Theory. https://nursing-theory.org/famous-nurses/Helen-Fairchild.php

Lawrence of Arabia. Arab warfare. Tactics. (n.d.). Pbs.org. https://www.pbs.org/lawrenceofarabia/revolt/warfare3.html

Lawrence of Arabia. Desert survival. Lawrence's description of a Bedouin feast. (n.d.). Pbs.org. https://www.pbs.org/lawrenceofarabia/revolt/food2.html

Lawrence of Arabia. Prince Feisal. (n.d.). Pbs.org. https://www.pbs.org/lawrenceofarabia/players/feisal.html

Lawrence of Arabia: The man behind the robes. (n.d.-a). Nam.ac.uk. https://www.nam.ac.uk/explore/lawrence-arabia-man-behind-robes

Lawrence of Arabia: The man behind the robes. (n.d.-b). Nam.ac.uk. https://www.nam.ac.uk/explore/lawrence-arabia-man-behind-robes

Leadership lessons from the Red Baron. (n.d.). Ramstein Air Base. https://www.ramstein.af.mil/News/Commentaries/Display/Article/305692/leadership-lessons-from-the-red-baron/

Lo Wang, H. (2014, April 1). The Harlem Hellfighters: Fighting Racism in the Trenches of WWI. NPR. https://www.npr.org/sections/codeswitch/2014/04/01/294913379/the-harlem-hellfighters-fighting-racism-in-the-trenches-of-wwi

Manfred von Richthofen biographie. (n.d.). Uni-stuttgart.de. https://www.hi.uni-stuttgart.de/wgt/ww-one/Start/Bleed_White/Military_Pilots/term_17399.html

Manfred von Richthofen. (n.d.). Newworldencyclopedia.org. https://www.newworldencyclopedia.org/entry/Manfred_von_Richthofen

Murphy, S. (n.d.). Lighthouse Girl, by Dianne Wolfer. Aussiereviews.com. https://aussiereviews.com/2009/08/lighthouse-girl-by-dianne-wolfer/

National Museum of the United States Army. (n.d.). Thenmusa.Org. https://www.thenmusa.org/biographies/alvin-c-york/

No.80 Squadron. (n.d.). Nationalcoldwarexhibition.org. https://www.nationalcoldwarexhibition.org/research/squadrons/80/

Patrick, B. K. (2017, August 30). Army nurse's letters draw attention to corps during World War I. Military.com. https://www.military.com/history/army-nurse-helen-fairchild.html

Red baron. (2009, November 9). HISTORY. https://www.history.com/topics/world-war-i/manfred-baron-von-richthofen

Schlitz, H. (2018, November 12). The Real Red Baron. College of Liberal Arts & Sciences at Illinois. https://las.illinois.edu/news/2018-11-12/real-red-baron

South African Air aces 1939-1945 - south African military history society. (n.d.). Samilitaryhistory.org. http://samilitaryhistory.org/vol013dt.html

Stilwell, B. (2020, October 23). "The Black Swallow of Death" was an American hero of France and the first black fighter pilot. Military.com. https://www.military.com/history/black-swallow-of-death-was-american-hero-of-france-and-first-black-fighter-pilot.html

Swopes, B. (n.d.). Marmaduke Thomas St. John pattle. Thisdayinaviation.com. https://www.thisdayinaviation.com/tag/marmaduke-thomas-st-john-pattle/

T. E. Lawrence and the art of war in the twenty-first century. (2011, July 13). The History Reader. https://www.thehistoryreader.com/military-history/t-e-lawrence-art-war-twenty-first-century/

Tarver Reviewed work :, L. (1978). In Wisdom's House: T. E. Lawrence in the Near East. Fu-berlin.de. https://blogs.fu-berlin.de/expertsandknowledges/files/2011/10/260210.pdf

The Girl on Breaksea Island : Archive page : The University of Western Australia. (n.d.). Edu.au. https://www.news.uwa.edu.au/archive/201411097126/girl-breaksea-island/

The lighthouse girl. (2019, December 10). Issuu. https://issuu.com/aust-maritime-safety-authority/docs/amsa_working_boats_october_2019_digital/s/158514

The New York Times. (1964, September 3). Sergeant York, War Hero, Dies; Killed 25 Germans and Captured 132 in the Argonne Battle. The New York Times. https://www.nytimes.com/1964/09/03/archives/sergeant-york-war-hero-dies-killed-25-germans-and-captured-132-in.html

The real Fay. (2016, April 16). Diannewolfer. https://diannewolfer.com/books/historical-fiction/lighthouse-girl/the-real-fay/

The Red Baron Tells All. (2022, October 20). HistoryNet. https://www.historynet.com/the-red-baron-tells-all/

The Taking of Akaba - 1917 - T.e. Lawrence, Auda abu tayi, Prince Feisal, port of Aqaba. (n.d.). Cliohistory.org. https://www.cliohistory.org/thomas-lawrence/akaba

Victoria Cross: Lance Corporal Albert Jacka, 14 Battalion, AIF. (n.d.). Gov.Au. https://www.awm.gov.au/collection/C94174

World War I. (2009, October 29). HISTORY. https://www.history.com/topics/world-war-i/world-war-i-history

WWII Post-traumatic Stress. (2020, June 26). The National WWII Museum | New Orleans; The National World War II Museum. https://www.nationalww2museum.org/war/articles/wwii-post-traumatic-stress

Captain Noel Chavasse (VC and Bar, MC) remembered. (n.d.). National Museums Liverpool. https://www.liverpoolmuseums.org.uk/stories/captain-noel-chavasse-vc-and-bar-mc-remembered

He who would true valor see. (n.d.). Churchtimes.co.uk. https://www.churchtimes.co.uk/articles/2017/1-september/faith/faith-features/he-who-would-true-valour-see

Hemmings, J. (2019, January 10). The incredible captain Noel Chavasse: One of the few men to be awarded the Victoria Cross twice. Warhistoryonline; War History Online. https://www.warhistoryonline.com/instant-articles/captain-noel-chavasse-ww1.html

IOC. (n.d.). Noel Godfrey CHAVASSE. Olympics.com. https://olympics.com/en/athletes/noel-godfrey-chavasse

Life story: Noel Godfrey Chavasse. (n.d.). Org.uk. https://livesofthefirstworldwar.iwm.org.uk/lifestory/787483

Noel Chavasse. (2019, February 25). The Royal British Legion. https://www.britishlegion.org.uk/stories/the-only-vc-and-bar-of-the-first-world-war

Private papers of Captain N G Chavasse VC* MC. (n.d.). Imperial War Museums. https://www.iwm.org.uk/collections/item/object/1030019940

(n.d.). The RAMC association - 1916 - Captain Noel Godfrey CHAVASSE. Org. uk. https://www.ramcassociation.org.uk/medical-vc-recipient-categories/47-ww1/227-1916-captain-noel-godfrey-chavasse

www.ingramcontent.com/pod-product-compliance
Lightning Source LLC
Chambersburg PA
CBHW060253150626
46553CB00019BA/2223